Peacemaking Christians

The Future of Just Wars, Pacifism, and
Nonviolent Resistance

Peacemaking Christians

The Future of Just Wars, Pacifism, and
Nonviolent Resistance

Michael K. Duffey

Sheed & Ward
Kansas City

Sheed & Ward™ is a service of The National Catholic Reporter Publishing Company.

———————————————◆———————————————

Library of Congress Cataloguing-in-Publication Data

Duffey, Michael K., 1948-
    Peacemaking Christians : the future of just wars, pacifism, and nonviolent resistance / Michael K. Duffey.
        p.   cm.
    Includes index.
    ISBN 1-55612-764-2 (pbk. : alk. paper)
    1. Peace—Religious aspects—Christianity. 2. War—Religious aspects—Christianity. 3. Pacifism—Religious aspects—Christianity. 4. Nonviolence—Religious aspects—Christianity. I. Title.
BT736.4.D84   1995
241.6242—dc20   95-14284
                                                                         CIP

———————————————◆———————————————

Published by: Sheed & Ward
                115 E. Armour Blvd.
                P.O. Box 419492
                Kansas City, MO 64141-6492

To order, call: (800) 333-7373

Cover design by Emil Antonucci.

Contents

Introduction v

1. A Christian Theology of Peace 1
   Introduction 1
   1. Peace: God's Gift and Our Task 3
   2. Faith, Hope, Love, Patience, and Humility 10
   Conclusion: Peace as a Healing and a Political Process . 14

2. When Is War Justified? The Criteria of Just Cause,
   Right Authority, and Right Intention 18
   Introduction 18
   1. Just Cause: A Contemporary Case Study 21
   2. War Against Iraq: By Whose Authority? 30
   3. Could War Have Been Prevented? 36

3. When Is War Justified? The Criteria of Proportionality,
   Success, and Last Resort 39
   Introduction 39
   1. Last Resort 40
   2. Strategic Proportionality 44
   3. The Probability of Success and Prospect of Peace . . 47

4. How is War to Be Justly Conducted? The Criteria of
   Civilian Immunity and Proportionality in Battle . . . 52
   Introduction 52
   1. The War against Iraq and Iraqi Civilians 55
   2. Desert Storm and the Criterion of Proportionality . . 64
   Conclusion: Will Old Principles Restrain New Wars? . 71

5. Is Just War an Effective Theory with which
   to Limit Conflict? 75
   Introduction 75
   Conclusion 86

6. Christian Pacifism (Reconsidered) 89
   Introduction 89
   1. Pacifism in Contemporary Catholicism 90
   2. Beyond the Caricatures: Pacifism Reconsidered . . . 102
   Conclusion 109

7. Christian Nonviolent Resistance 113
   Introduction 113
   1. Poland 116
   2. East Germany, 1981-1989 124
   3. The Philippines: The Nonviolent Revolution of 1986 . 129
   Conclusion: The Lessons of Nonviolent Resistance . . 134

8. The Peacemaking Church 143
   Introduction 143
   1. Passing on a Peace Tradition 145
   2. "Make Me an Instrument of Your Peace" 151
   Conclusion 158

Note to Educators 164

Index 168

Introduction

THE LITERATURE ON PEACE AND WAR IS ENORMOUS. THE SHELVES
are bulging with books on the subject from philosophical and
theological perspectives. Even more has been written by political theorists. Psychologists and anthropologists have also had
plenty to say about war and violence. Nonetheless, while many
books have made important contributions to clarifying how
war and peace have been viewed and experienced in the western tradition, they are not widely read. Many are of an academic nature, interpreting aspects of the tradition and debating
various theories for an audience of fellow professionals.

This book is a theological examination of peace and war
as understood in Christian moral teaching. In this sense it, too,
is specialized. It will survey three identifiable positions within
the Christian tradition: the just-war doctrine, pacifism, and
nonviolent resistance. My confessional focus will be the Roman
Catholic Church and how its views on war, peace, and conflict
resolution have developed during this century. In this exposi-
tion, I have attempted to place important issues before the
reader while aiming at clarification rather than simplification
of the ongoing debates about these traditions. I am apprecia-
tive of the excellent studies that are available on the history of
Christian thought and practice on these subjects. This book re-
lies on the fruit of these historical projects but does not offer a
historical survey.

Although peace and war have been subjected to much examination, critical study seems to have had little impact on public attitudes about war and violence. Two pervasive convictions about war and violence seem to preempt the discussion. The first is a profound "realism" that supposes war and violence to be inevitable. The second is a profound cynicism that contends war and violence are profitable and thus desirable for the power elite. Both attitudes have the effect of dismissing further moral evaluation. If war is predetermined, then we have little freedom to control the impulses that lead to it. Equally, if it is good for business, our moral nostrums will not be able to prevent or restrain warmaking.

While the subjects of peace, war, and violence have long been of personal and professional interest to me, this particular study had its beginning during the Persian Gulf War. After Iraq invaded Kuwait it drew nearly unanimous condemnation from the rest of the world. The U.N. then passed strong resolutions against Iraq and the U.S. organized a coalition of nations. As the threat of war escalated, U.S. Catholic Bishops publicly stated their conclusions that the conditions for a morally justifiable war had not been met. But war came and President Bush declared it a "just war." Although the language of just-war was uttered by both those who opposed war and those who supported it, public discussion on the morality of military force was not very deep. Within the Catholic community, the laity received little guidance from their pastors. In step with 90% of the American people, Catholics and most other Christian denominations supported the war effort, even though a week earlier, 45% of those polled wanted to give sanctions more time to work. During the war, technical explanations of how laser-guided missiles dominated the mass media. Moral discussion of Operation Desert Storm was neither invited nor heard.

A year after the war, I introduced an undergraduate ethics class to the just-war tradition. The students had read about war from the point of view of several U.S. soldiers who had served in Vietnam. They had also read about the valiant and successful nonviolent efforts of a community of French Christians to rescue Jews during the Nazi era. After offering an explanation of the logic of the just-war criteria, I invited my students to evaluate the Gulf War in light of them. Most decided that the war was justly undertaken and justly conducted. A few students criticized the war. But neither the majority nor the minority offered strong arguments for their conclusions. Our attempted "public debate" about war was disappointing for its lack of any critical edge. The results were disturbing. Although students told me that our unit on the morality of war had sensitized them as never before to the destructive consequences of war for all involved, it bothered me that the just-war tradition had apparently failed to make them ask critical moral questions about the very costly war they had recently witnessed.

I concluded that the Catholic community and other Christian denominations need to pay much better attention to their own traditions regarding just-war and pacifism. They also need to become more aware of the theory and practice of nonviolent resistance presently flowering in Christian communities today. While President Reagan's "tough talk" regarding the Soviet Union often made headlines, the more significant story is still largely unknown. That story is about the nonviolent resistance undertaken by Eastern Europe Christian communities which helped bring about freedom, greater justice, and reduced the threat of nuclear war. In sum, the Catholic community needs to announce with more confidence the Gospel of peace and strengthen its witness to the ways of peace. Peacemaking should not be relegated merely to ecclesial "justice and peace" committees.

The book proceeds as follows. Chapter One outlines a theology of peace affirming the divine attributes of compassion, mercy, and forgiveness. It explores the call of Christians both to be reconciled and to be reconcilers, and it considers the task of the church, the nonviolent community of Jesus' disciples. The Church has historically sought to impose restraints on war. Its chief vehicle for doing so has been the just-war theory. For this reason, Chapters Two, Three, and Four describe the conditions that must be met for war to be morally permissible under just-war criteria. The Persian Gulf War of 1990-1991 serves as a case study for the application of the 8 just-war criteria.

Chapter Two examines the criteria of just cause, right intention, and legitimate authority. I consider the history of the conflict that led up to Iraq's invasion of Kuwait as well as the Coalition's response in terms of ten stated objectives. I also consider the intention of the Bush Administration by observing its response to the crisis. Finally, I consider what did *not* happen: the enforcing of U.N. resolutions demanding Iraq's withdrawal from Kuwait *without* the use of military force.

Chapter Three raises the issues of proportionality, probability of success, and last resort in light of what happened during the Gulf War. Was the price of liberating Kuwait too great in terms of Iraqi lives and the destruction of Iraqi society? What would the "peace" look like after the Coalition prevailed? What options short of resorting to war might have induced Saddam Hussein to recall his forces from Kuwait? As difficult as such questions are to answer ahead of time, they demanded more serious consideration than they received.

Chapter Four examines the most troubling moral questions raised by the Gulf War. While not directly targeted, civilians suffered considerable harm during (and long after) the war because of the destruction of Iraq's infrastructure. The coalition's swift and decisive military victory was aptly characterized as "desert slaughter." My conclusion is that the two criteria governing the conduct of war — namely, civilian immunity and proportionality — were seriously violated in the Gulf War.

Chapter Five considers the future of the doctrine of justifiable war by considering its present status in Catholic teaching. I argue that if the doctrine is to have future usefulness in offering moral guidance, its criteria must be specified more clearly and restrictively than they currently are. Furthermore, I suggest that the conflicts in Somalia and Bosnia may have important lessons to teach us about the limits of military force.

Chapter Six considers the refusal on the part of some early Christians to take up arms and the pluralism of attitudes toward war and military service that arose in early Christianity. By the fourth century, if not earlier, pacifism was the minority position within Christianity. I will argue that much common ground exists between pacifism and the just-war doctrine which has dominated Catholic thinking on the morality of war for many centuries. My conclusion is that despite the strong cultural bias against pacifism, Christianity can make a strong case for it.

Chapter Seven examines the least explored response to war and peace, the practice of nonviolent resistance. Akin to pacifism in some respects and just-war convictions in others, nonviolent resistance has become a widespread practice in this century. It has been embraced by Christian communities (and endorsed by Church leaders) with considerable success, especially in the past three decades. This chapter tells the stories of the contributions of nonviolent resistance to peace in Eastern Europe and the Philippines. My suspicion is that a Catholic debate that gets stuck on "just-war versus pacifism" misses an inspired moment in which Christian communities are bringing the peace of Christ to bear in bleak situations by learning the disciplines of forgiveness and reconciliation.

Chapter Eight broadens our analysis of conflict and violence, examining the relationship between military force and the growing violence in U.S. society. What can the churches do to foster peace and cure our violence? This concluding chapter challenges us personally to address the issue of violence and to commit ourselves to peacemaking.

This book is more than a survey of differing Christian attitudes toward peace and war, for it develops an argument along the way. The argument is this. From very early in the tradition, Christians held conflicting views about whether they were ever permitted to engage in war. Over the centuries a strategy for restraining both the recourse to war and the conduct of war developed in the form of the just-war theory. That tradition is now in trouble unless its several conditions for making war morally permissible can be shored up. All Christian churches are by definition "peace churches." One way of being such is to affirm that pacifism is not a marginal position but a mainstream one for Christians to hold. Another way of witnessing to its essential peacemaking vocation is for the church to apply the lessons of creative nonviolent resistance being practiced by Catholic and Protestant communities in the many cultural contexts in which the church announces the peace of Christ.

I would like to acknowledge the contributions made by three graduate assistants. Ms. Ginny Richards and Sr. Reneé Mirkes gathered research on the Gulf War. Mr. Jim Keane made many helpful editorial suggestions during the writing process.

The prayer that accompanies this book is that people everywhere may be freed from the pain and sorrow of violence and war.

—Michael K. Duffey

Peacemaking Christians

The Future of Just Wars, Pacifism, and
Nonviolent Resistance

CHAPTER ONE

A Christian Theology of Peace

Introduction

As Jesus prepared to take leave of his disciples, he consoled them, saying: "Peace I leave with you, my own peace I give to you" (Jn 14:27). He promised to send his Spirit upon them that they might realize the "peace that the world cannot give." What is this peace that Jesus intends for us? Can we really know what that peace is beyond a present yearning, an aspiration for that which we do not yet possess? We yearn for the soothing of human passions that lead to cruelty and killing. We yearn for humane ways of existing together so that people can be genuinely cared for and comforted. In short, we yearn for our innermost souls and our outermost social structures to be pacified by the goodness of God.

It is the task of all who proclaim the Gospel of Christ to make Christ's peace manifest to the world. What Christians — and members of other religious traditions as well — bring to the task is the belief that peace is possible because peace is God's will and therefore must become our way of being in the world. In this chapter we reflect upon the divine gift of peace as a duty of Christians in a conflict-filled world. Section One summarizes the theology of peace that the U.S. Catholic Bishops outlined in their 1983 pastoral letter, *The Challenge of Peace*. Reflection on peace takes us to the center of Christian affirmations about God, about Christ, and about the community of

1

faith, the church. These beliefs form the foundation of a theology of peace. Section Two explores peace in the pattern of the Christian moral life. Finally, the chapter concludes with a consideration of the insights of one of the most respected peace theologians of our time, Fr. Bernard Häring.

The rest of the book will consider how Christians have endeavored to build peace and resolve conflict through both just-war moral reasoning and pacifist commitments. As we shall see, Roman Catholics have sought peace by a number of pathways. Since the time of Augustine the Church has made serious efforts to limit the destruction of war. These efforts have been handed down by means of the "just-war tradition": a set of criteria to be reflected upon both before and during the course of war. As we shall see in the chapters ahead, the 1991 Gulf War serves as a prime example of just-war theory's inability to restrain the destructive effects of modern warfare. I shall argue that the lesson of the Gulf War is that the just-war path to peace is fraught with hazards. Thus, in the face of modern warfare, Catholicism must travel other paths to peace.

Modern Catholicism has reaffirmed pacifism, recognizing that pacifism is far from passivity. As we shall see in later chapters, pacifist commitments promote peace by active nonviolent resistance to injustice. Indeed, the Christian presumption against the use of violence is being most effectively expressed in nonviolent movements. In 1993 alone, some thirteen nonviolent campaigns occurred throughout the world. All but one of them was successful. Communities have discovered that nonviolent methods are a powerful force against injustice — and the only effective means of overcoming deadly cycles of fear, mistrust, and retaliation.

For Christians, however, nonviolence must be more than a tactic. It must be a way of life nourished by a theology of peace. The present chapter will outline the contours of such a theology. Then we will explore the Gulf War as an example of the limitations of the just-war tradition in curbing the destructiveness of modern warfare. We will then trace the recent developments within Catholicism toward the pacifist position before providing an account of contemporary nonviolent movements among Christians.

1. Peace: God's Gift and Our Task

Over a decade ago the U.S. Catholic Bishops offered a vision of peace. Peace, they said, is a gift of God's very self offered to those who open themselves to receiving it. Peace is the fruit of "a right relationship with God." As the Genesis account of creation affirms, all things were once at peace insofar as they existed in harmony and wholeness and were rightly related to their Maker. But this original harmony was rent by disorder at the hands of rebellious creatures. Peace was shattered by human beings who no longer "rightly related to God" and had grown suspicious, fearful, envious and, finally, murderous.

But God's gift of peace was offered anew. God promised to restore the original harmony and wholeness of creation. The biblical writers proclaim the coming restoration of peace. In Genesis 12 a story unfolds of how God plans to reestablish the harmony of creation and save human beings from the death sentence they have imposed on themselves. The stories of the covenant that God initiated with Abraham and Sarah and their descendants form a dialectic of divine promise of the restoration of peace and of the human obligation to make peace a reality. With the promise comes a task, conveyed by Yahweh through Moses:

> If you obey the commandments of Yahweh your God that I [Moses] enjoin on you today, if you love Yahweh your God and follow his ways . . . you will live and increase, and Yahweh your God will bless you in that land which you are entering to make your own. (Dt.30:15-16)

Essentially two commandments were enjoined on the Israelites: they must be faithful to Yahweh and they must establish justice in their midst and extend compassion to all persons, especially the "least" among them. If they do these things they will live in peace and be blessed with prosperity.

Israel's commandments are intended to restore "right relations" — that is, peace — with God and between human beings. For both the peoples of the Old Testament and later of the New Testament, the right relationships to which human beings are called are summed up in the double commands: "love God with your whole heart, mind and soul, and love your neighbor as yourself."

When Israel was conquered by foreign powers its prophets blamed the nation itself for its woes: Israel had not kept the terms of the covenant. Israel had no peace because it had failed to practice justice and mercy by spurning the cry of the widow, the orphan, the poor, and the stranger. The "right relationship" and the salvation offered by God was spurned by the refusal of the people to establish a right relationship with one another.

The longing of Israel for fulfillment and salvation increasingly fixed upon a "messiah" whose coming would signal the restoration of Israel's peace with God. Later, Christians conferred the title of messiah on Jesus, "the one in whom the fullness of God was pleased to dwell, who made peace by the blood of the Cross" (Colossians 1: 19-20). New Testament scholars point out that the implications of Jesus' teachings — and particularly those contained in the Sermon on the Mount — can be understood only by referring back to the kind of messiah envisioned by the prophet Isaiah. The "Servant Song" (Is. 40-55), composed during the Exile in the mid-sixth century, B.C.E., describes God's emissary who will restore right relations/justice upon the earth. This messianic figure is described:

> Here is my servant whom I uphold,
> My chosen one in whom my soul delights
> I have endowed him with my spirit
> that he may bring true justice to the nations.
>
> He does not cry out or shout aloud,
> or make his voice heard in the streets.

He does not break the crushed reed,
nor quench the wavering flame.

Faithfully he brings true justice;
he will neither waver, nor be crushed
until true justice is established on earth. . . . (42:1-4)

Not by a show of strength but in apparent weakness will Yahweh's Servant bring divine justice and judgment, liberation and healing to the world. His power is not found in awesome or intimidating force; on the contrary, he submits to suffering, and by such humility and submission before evildoers he saves others. His suffering is redemptive: "He was pierced for our transgressions, tortured for our iniquities; the chastisement he bore is health for us, and by his scourging we are healed" (Is. 53:5). The servant of Yahweh prevails over violence and brings justice.

The U.S. Catholic Bishops center their theology of peace and of peacemaking on "the unique revelation of God that is Jesus Christ and of the reign of God which Jesus proclaimed and inaugurated" (39). In Mark's gospel Jesus announced his mission: "The time is fulfilled, and the kingdom of God is at hand; repent, and believe the good news" (Mk. 1:15). The "good news" and the "Kingdom of God" are closely identified with the restoration of wholeness and harmony long desired by Israel. Jesus calls his hearers to prepare for the fullness of the Kingdom by committing themselves to a new way of life marked by a willingness "to forgive those who trespass against" them. The Bishops exhort us to seek "a right relationship with God" by continuously seeking opportunities for "forgiveness, reconciliation, and union" between human beings. "The forgiveness of God," they say, "is manifested in communal forgiveness and mercy" (46).

The conditions for entering the Kingdom are nowhere more eloquently stated than in the various versions of Jesus' Sermon on the Mount. In these teachings, Jesus exhorts his followers to practice forgiveness and to pray for those who persecute them. He urges them to love their enemies and to resist repaying evildoers with evil. What is so extraordinary about Jesus' love command is precisely his teaching regarding enemies. "Turning the other cheek," "going the second mile," and "giving one's cloak" run counter to our natural instincts. Yet, as Dorothy Weaver observes,

> Jesus paradoxically holds out to the community of disciples a power they have never before experienced, the power to act in the face of evil. This is Jesus' answer to the "law of retaliation."[1]

In his parable about the demands of love, Jesus does not permit his Jewish hearers to classify Samaritans as enemies any longer but holds one of them up as a model of practical and unselfish love of neighbor. The distinguishing characteristic of Jesus' teaching on love is that it is "being constructively and compassionately extended to the enemy."[2] Those who love their enemies in this way will mark the peacemakers whom Jesus says "shall be called sons and daughters of God."

The kingdom and the peace Jesus announced were not relegated to some distant future. Indeed, they were powerfully present in Jesus himself. New Testament scholar Rudolf Schnackenburg underscores the wedding of the present and the future prospects of peace in Jesus, the herald of peace:

> Jesus did not only announce the coming reign of God, but made clear in his message and his actions that the reign of God already was breaking in full of promise and effectiveness, that it was becoming visible symbolically in his own deeds, healings, assurance of forgiveness, turning toward the poor, the disregarded, and the oppressed. The rule of God is already now a discernible reality and places on his hearers of the gospel the urgent appeal to conduct themselves accordingly.[3]

1. Dorothy Jean Weaver, "Transforming Nonresistance," in *Love of Enemy and Nonretaliation in the New Testament*, Willard Swartley, ed. (Louisville: Westminster, 1992), 56.

2. Victor Paul Furnish, *The Love Command in the New Testament* (Nashville: Abingdon, 1972), 62-63.

3. Rudolf Schnackenburg, *Die Bergpredigt: Utopische Vision oder Handlungsan-weisung* (Düsseldorf: Patmos Verlag, 1982), 56-57.

Jesus suffered rejection, persecution, and death for the sake of the kingdom. The bishops affirm that "Jesus' message and his actions were dangerous ones [that] led to his death," and acknowledge that he "refused to defend himself with force or with violence"(49). Yet Jesus' resurrection confirms the victory of divine love over sin and death and is a source of courage for Christians to commit themselves to the practice of justice and of mercy and to risk taking initiatives for peace. Jesus reassures those who must suffer for the sake of restoring the Kingdom that their "reward will be great."

The New Testament proclaims a messiah with the disarming commands to love one's enemies and to pray for one's persecutors. Jesus' example of nonretaliation challenges the presumption that violence is necessary to establish justice and preserve peace. The New Testament revelation about Jesus also challenges our assumptions about the ways of God.

Heinrich Spaemann puts it forcefully:

> Jesus is nonviolent because God is nonviolent. God does not force, but shows trust; he sets free and guides to freedom. . . . Nonviolence, just as much as poverty, belongs to the mystery of the Redeemer and redemption. The test is whether one shares in that mystery.[4]

Indeed, there are a variety of images of God in the scriptures, especially in the Hebrew scriptures. For instance, in the biblical stories that relate the history of Israel before the Babylonian exile (i.e., 12th to 6th century, B.C.E.), God appears as a warrior and executioner. A frequent theme in the oldest Israelite literature is Yahweh's destruction of Israel's enemies.

In the Psalms, one hears the psalmist alternately pleading for protection of Israel and offering songs of thanksgiving for victories won and enemies vanquished. While the occasion is one of praising God's loving kindness, the divine personality nonetheless appears to be violent and vindictive. In the use of psalms for liturgical prayer, the Church avoids passages that

---

4. Heinrich Spaemann, "Die Stunde der Gewaltlosigkeit," in *Geist und Leben* 57 (1984), 84.

depict God as vindictive and destructive — passages such as: "He struck down the first-born of Egypt, his love is everlasting! He slaughtered famous kings, his love is everlasting!" (Ps. 136) and "Destructive Daughter of Babylon . . . a blessing on him who takes and dashes your babies against the rock!" (Ps. 137).

Such images appear to identify violence as an attribute of God and to legitimize human violence as sometimes divinely ordained. But such conclusions rely on uncritical interpretations of biblical texts.[5] Scholars take issue with the common assumption that war was an instrument of divine judgment. Scholars who have examined the "holy war" tradition in the biblical narratives suggest that they were understood differently by their authors than by modern hearers. Lohfink reaches the conclusion that

> in the priestly historiography war does not exist. We do not find in it the slightest indication of "holy wars" and/or of divine commands to slaughter whole populations.[6]

Many biblical historians agree that the image of Yahweh as warrior was a primitive image that eventually receded from Israel's religious consciousness.[7]

---

5. For example, Israel's war stories involving the mass slaughter of its enemies may be read as historical accounts of actual events. But Old Testament scholar Norbert Lohfink observes that the writer of the deuteronomic history does not interpret premeditated slaughter of whole populations either as an actual happening or as a divine command. Lohfink contends that the Hebrew tribes' "conquest" of Canaan, for example, was "only the expulsion of the ruling class of Canaanite cities, the downfall of domineering societies and the political systems." *Gewalt und Gewaltlosigkeit im Alten Testament*, Frieburg im Br. 1983, 59.

6. Lohfink, 76. Especially significant, in this regard, is the research into the causes and consequences of violence by René Girard, professor of comparative culture and literature. Girard's theories have influenced contemporary biblical scholarship.

7. Lohfink observes that the Old Testament came from "a still violent world" but that it gradually "unmasked and denounced violence and has projected its being overcome." Noting that the early Israelite religious and cultural environment reflected the association between violence and the sacred,

The Catholic bishops note that the warrior image of God was "gradually transformed, particularly after the experience of the exile, when God was no longer identified with military victory and might" (30) but with healing and redemption.

However, despite this transformation of the image of the divine in the religious consciousness of Israel, the Warrior-God image persists even today — alongside the belief that human warfare serves God's purposes in history and that wars are God's judgment on evildoers.

At the very center of the exhortations of the U.S. Catholic Bishops for Christians to be peacemakers is their endorsement of nonviolence as the most faithful way of proclaiming the Lordship of Jesus Christ and of advancing his kingdom. They affirm unequivocally: "We believe [that] work to develop non-violent means of fending off aggression and resolving conflict best reflects the call of Jesus to love and to justice" (78). Theologian Rudolf Pesch exhorts contemporary Christians to imitate the spirit of the New Testament communities by construing "the death of Christ as the hour of birth of a nonviolent society of the people of God in the New Covenant."[8] Nonviolently struggling to overcome injustice and alienation is synonymous with being a disciple of Jesus. The Bishops say:

> As disciples and as children of God, it is our task to seek for ways in which to make the forgiveness, justice and mercy and love of God visible in a world where violence and enmity are too often the norm. When we listen to God's word, we hear again and always the call to repentance and to belief: to repentance because although we are redeemed we continue to need redemp-

---

he writes:
> Theological exaltation of wars and victories is not an invention of Israel . . . Stories that the "sacred awe" was decisive in battle and that God was the one who enacted everything were at hand from its beginning, including the thought that the deity can turn in wrath against its own people. (Lohfink, 59)

8.   N. Lohfink and Rudolf Pesch, *Weltgestaltung und Gewaltlosigkeit*, p. 67.

tion; to belief, because although the reign of God is near, it is still seeking its fullness. (55)

Peacemaking nonviolently is a continuous "inner" and "outer" struggle. Our own inner hostilities must be transformed before we can effectively overcome interpersonal conflicts.

2. Faith, Hope, Love, Patience, and Humility

What kind of characteristics need to be nurtured in us as members of the church if we are to effectively carry the Gospel of peace to the world? St. Paul summarized the essential qualities of the Christian life, when he wrote to the Corinthians:

Love is always patient and kind . . . love is never boastful . . . love takes no pleasure in other people's sins but delights in the truth; it is always ready to excuse, to trust, to hope, and to endure whatever comes. . . . In short, there are three things that last: faith, hope and love; and the greatest of these is love. (I Cor. 13:4-7,13)

Faith is confidence that God's goodness and love are more powerful than the enmity and alienation that now shatters our world. Faith is dependency, moment by moment, on the graciousness of God who is giver of life and salvation, and is ever compassionate and merciful. Faith is willingness to abide with the One who is present in his Son's suffering and who "makes justice shine" (Is. 42:1) by means of compassion and mercy. Commitment to nonviolence is our deepest exercise of faith in the God of Jesus Christ.

The virtue of *hope* enables us to persevere in a nonviolent way of life. Hopeful people are able to carry on the struggle to transform society despite apparent defeats. However, they are sustained by more than blind optimism. Jürgen Moltmann insists that for people of faith, "hope alone is realistic . . . because it alone takes seriously the possibilities with which all reality is fraught."[9] Hope enables people of faith to imagine the transformation of oppressive social, political, and economic orders, precisely because they firmly believe that the "old order" is passing away in favor of the "new order" of God's reign. Martin Luther King, Jr., paraphrased Jesus' saying "I have come not to bring peace, but the sword" this way: "Whenever I come, a conflict is precipitated between the old and the new. . . . I have come to bring a positive peace which is the presence of justice, love, yea, even the Kingdom of God."[10] King's ability to hope that the old order of racial segregation would give way to a new order of equality, freedom, and justice for people of all color arose from his faith in the God of love and justice. Hope was his sword in the battle against the passivity of accepting an unjust order. A Christian hope like King's disturbs the status quo. So confident is such hope that it refuses to use violence against the old order. King courageously agitated for the new order. But his faith and his hope made him able to suffer the violence of men fearful and desperate to maintain the old order.[11]

The virtue of *love* marks the fullness of life because through love we experience God's redemptive power most fully. "God so loved the world," writes John, "that he gave his only son that those who believe in him might have life." St. Paul proclaims that we are healed by the wounds of Jesus, God's servant and son. The essence of love is participation in the divine healing of enemies, the transforming of the estranged into friends, and the redeeming of human beings from the variety of hatreds that imprison them. To love is to cooperate in Jesus' healing and reconciling of the world. To love is to participate in the progressive coming of the reign of God. In situations of stubborn injustice, proclaiming love may require the endurance of unearned suffering. By our participation in Jesus' suffering we are become part of his healing presence in

---

9. Jürgen Moltmann, *Theology of Hope* (New York: Harper and Row, 1967), 25.

10. Martin Luther King, Jr., *Stride Toward Freedom* (New York: Harper and Row, 1958), 40.

11. In *Stride Toward Freedom* King described the violent efforts of segregationists to kill black hopes by means of fear.

the world. Christians do not want the cup of suffering. Yet they desire to overcome injustice and heal hostilities so much that they are willing to travel the way of suffering.

Other virtues are also characteristic of the Christian life. Two of them are essential to being peacemakers: patience and humility. *Patience* is required in order to persevere amidst adversity without succumbing to fear or resorting to fanaticism. Patience means resisting the urge to "make things turn out right" by corrupt or destructive means. But patience is not passivity. Civil rights activists frequently were told that they were seeking "too much too soon" and were advised to slow down. In 1962 King replied to such charges from a group of white clergymen while in a Birmingham jail. Quoting an American jurist, that "justice too long delayed is justice denied," King urged blacks to be radically impatient with conditions that denied them their birthright of self-respect; to tolerate oppression is to cooperate in evil. Authentic patience is the determination to resist evil actively but without violent means.

Transforming attitudes and structures often requires extraordinary persistence. Being patient is often painfully learned: instead of results — coming quickly and unambiguously — we learn to be faithful to God's power.

Humility is the capacity to seek truth beyond one's own current possession of it. Humility disposes us to openness and cooperation with others, especially toward those we are not likely to want to listen to. Authentic humility has nothing to do with passively accepting humiliation. It is recognition of one's own limitations.

These virtues empower us to be peacemakers. The epistle to the Ephesians uses a military metaphor to call Christians to a life of unflagging love and service:

> So stand your ground, with truth buckled around your waist, and integrity for a breastplate, wearing for shoes on your feet the eagerness to spread the gospel of peace and always carrying the shield of faith so that you can use it to put out the burning arrow of the evil one. And then you must accept salvation from God to

be your helmet and receive the word of God from the
Spirit to use as a sword. (Eph. 6:14-17)

The armaments of Christian peacemaking are the weapons of
the Spirit of God. They are more than enough to subdue the
forces of evil.

Theologian Glen Stassen has identified in the Sermon on
the Mount and in the Pauline epistles several practical and
concrete actions that form a basic pattern of Christian peacemaking. In outline form these peacemaking actions are:

(1) acknowledging our own alienation and need for God
(Matt. 5 on hypocrisy; Rom. 1:18 and 12:1 on grace)

(2) taking the first step to approach and talk with an adversary, seeking reconciliation (Luke 12:57-59)

(3) resisting the urge to take revenge; rather, take the first
initiative to overcome hostility (Matt. 5:38-39)

(4) working to remedy injustices that breed hostilities (Matt. 6)

(5) affirming an adversary's valid interests (Luke 6:27-28)

(6) praying for adversaries (Matt. 5:44; Rom. 12:12,14)

(7) forgoing judgments; instead forgiving — and repent for
our own mistakes (Matt. 7:1-5)

(8) joining with others in order to offer and receive mutual
support in the struggle to be peacemakers. (Matt. 7:28)[12]

These are the practical ways in which we move toward peace.

The last of the enumerated actions could also be listed
first, for it emphasizes the communal nature of the task. The
Christian churches announce the peace of Christ to the world
and exist to make that peace present. The U.S. Catholic Bishops write:

Because peace, like the kingdom of God itself, is both a
divine gift and a human work, the Church should con-
tinually pray for the gift and share in the work. We are

---

12. Stassen, *Just Peacemaking* (Louisville: Westminster/John Knox, 1992).
Chapters Two and Three.

> called to be a Church at the service of peace, precisely
> because peace is one manifestation of God's word and
> work in our midst. (23)

God's work and word are not yet fully manifested; the Kingdom of peace is still a promise unfulfilled. But the "not yet" of the present should not lead us to lose faith in the possibility of peace. Instead, the Christian community must faithfully seek to imitate Jesus' nonviolent liberation from the violence that oppresses both victims and perpetrators.

Conclusion: Peace as a Healing and a Political Process

A remarkable contribution to contemporary thinking about peacemaking comes from Fr. Bernard Häring. Fr. Häring is best known for his ethics textbooks which are widely used in Catholic universities and seminaries (He himself has taught seminarians in Rome for almost forty years). He is also a major Catholic contributor in the field of medical ethics. Häring speaks with the authority of one who has witnessed overwhelming violence. As a young Catholic priest, he was drafted into the army of the Third Reich in November, 1939. He was trained as a medic and then assigned to a German division in occupied France. Several months later, as Hitler's army moved east, Häring was ordered with his division to the Russian front. From October 1941, until he was wounded in May 1942, Fr. Häring treated the injured and offered the last rites to the dying, both Germans and Russians, during the fiercest battles of World War II. Few want peace more ardently than people like Fr. Häring, who have survived the horrors of war and cannot forget its images. In his later years he has addressed the issues of peace and nonviolence with particular vigor. In *The Healing Power of Peace and Nonviolence* (1985), he places peacemaking at the center of the Christian vocation.[13] He approaches violence as a pathological condition — an illness — for which peacemaking is a therapeutic activity. Häring

---

13. Bernard Häring, *The Healing Power of Peace and Nonviolence* (English publication: Mahwah, N.J.: Paulist Press, 1986), 7-9, 12-13.

notes some of the symptoms of the pathology that must be treated: enemy-images that fuel war, diversions of vast amounts of resources into military research and production, and the dangerous race for nuclear and conventional weapon superiority. Modern western culture, he asserts, is sick with violence. Its cure will not come about by lecturing the patient but only by applying healing methods. Häring is not just employing a medical analogy but is referring to a deeply rooted psychological condition. The cure he envisions will require three things: first, the resources of religious faith, beginning with the faith that we can be redeemed from violence; second, the political agenda of winning over those who form public opinion "to commit themselves to the cause of nonviolence and nonviolent defence,"[14] and third, small communities which will "learn more about nonviolence and train themselves for the cause."[15]

Fr. Häring's study of peacemaking offers both rich exploration of biblical scholarship and creative methods for the recovery of health and wholeness for individuals and society. His message is an imperative: seek the practical ways to bring about the healing power of peace and nonviolence or risk the progressive destruction of the conditions necessary for human existence.

Häring describes the comprehensive work of peace as transforming cultural, economic, and social relationships by recognizing oppositions and conflicts and working toward "the harmony of all energies of life."[16] Such harmonizing must occur through concrete processes of proposing and bargaining over difficult policies regarding defense and international security. It also requires serious investment in teaching and learning skills of conflict resolution at every level of society.

His vision and vocation of Christian peacemaking are indelibly marked by the senseless violence of our time. He tells

---

14. Häring, 108.

15. Häring, 108.

16. Häring, 8. Häring is quoting the Jewish writer Herman Cohen.

the story of a young German Jesuit seminarian who came to him the night before a terrible battle on the Russian front. The seminarian told him:

> I do not want to lose my life in this senseless business; I want to spend it for something worthwhile. When the war is over, there will be a great task ahead of us, as ministers of the Church, to serve people and to work for a better, freer world.[17]

The next day in battle, that young man was among the first to die, leaving to others the task of peacemaking. Häring has honored his memory by working to heal us of our violence. It remains the task of all those who cherish the memory of Jesus to bring his peace with a needy world by joining in the peacemaking ministry of his church.

The move from a "theology of peace" to "peace politics" may seem to be a jarring transition from religious considerations to secular strategies. However, as we move from a theology of peace to a politics of peace we are not changing the focus. We are intensifying it. We are moving to the next stage of the consideration: how peace is to be practiced. "Salvation" has to do with the progressive realization of God's reign in history. It is unavoidably "political" not because political programs will save us but because politics is the arena in which human communities struggle to create more just relationships. "Politics" often appears as a crass business in which power-grabbing, dishonesty, and betrayal of public trust is commonplace. But peacemaking must take place in the public arena. Peacemakers must contend with others who have equally strong interests. Also, Christian peacemakers must collaborate with others interested in their quest for peace. Thus, peacemaking is "political" and it often requires our participation in political processes.

---

17. Quoted by Bernard Häring in *Embattled Witness: Memories of a Time of War* (New York: Seabury Press, 1976), 5.

Questions for Reflection

1. What does the "Suffering Servant" in Isaiah achieve and how does he accomplish it?

2. What evidence in Jesus' life and teaching suggest that he embraced nonviolence?

3. What position do the U.S. Catholic Bishops take on nonviolence. Were you surprised? Why or why not?

4. While the Bishops articulated a theology of peace grounded in the Old and New Testaments, can you speculate why the Catholic church has not identified itself as a "peace church." Do you think that is changing?

5. Explain why each of the virtues we discussed is necessary to sustain us as peacemakers.

6. How is a "politics of peace" related to a "theology of peace"?

CHAPTER TWO

When Is War Justified? The Criteria of Just Cause, Right Authority, and Right Intention

Introduction

The "post-war era" that began in 1945 has hardly been an era of peace. Besides the Cold War that witnessed enormous build-ups of conventional and nuclear weapons between East and West, there have been well over a hundred "hot wars" around the world since 1945. Whether motivated by religion, nationalism, ideology, greed, or a combination of these, the results have been many seasons of violence and counter-violence contributing to human suffering and death of immense proportions. How have Christian churches attempted to promote peace in this century of war?

Catholic and Protestant leaders from around the world demonstrated one way of being peacemakers a decade ago when various Catholic Bishops' conferences and gatherings of the World Conferences of Churches condemned nuclear war, arms buildups, and warfighting strategies as violations of traditional criteria for "just-war." The anti-war stances of Catholic and Protestant pronouncements frequently appealed to a venerable tradition in the West that establishes conditions for justifiable war. The just-war tradition offers a moral framework both for judging the legitimacy of resorting to war and for evaluating wars after the fact. Clearly, the just-war tradition is not simply the province of Christian communities but has become common ground in the Western world for being critical about war. Its influence has become institutionalized to some degree in international laws and conventions regarding war and in codes of military conduct adopted by many nations.

Before examining how the just-war tradition was brought to bear in the Persian Gulf crisis, it is helpful to see how the tradition historically arose. The just-war theory can be traced to St Augustine in the later fourth century. The issue that was posed for Augustine was whether Christians, intent on preparing themselves for eternity, should concern themselves with the defense of the empire against barbarian invaders. Should Christians support and even serve in the armies of Rome battling barbarian forces threatening the *pax Romana*? Augustine believed that Christians could and should serve the cause of the empire's stability, which made possible the "acquisition of the necessities of life."[1] For Augustine, a harmonious and well-ordered society was also favorable to the evangelical mission of the Christian church. He considered the defense of the Roman world as ultimately the defense of the church. While these fruits of earthly peace were clearly of a lesser order than the ultimate peace of God for which we all await, these two goods were associated: the enjoyment of worldly peace permitted us to turn our attention to the ultimate peace for which we were created.

Augustine was asked by a Christian who commanded a Roman legion whether he ought not to resign. Augustine responded that the man could effectively practice love of neighbor by conscientiously defending the Empire against barbarians. Augustine counseled him to "be a peacemaker even in waging war so that by your conquest you may lead those you subdue to the enjoyment of peace."[2] But Augustine was not

---

1. St. Augustine, *The City of God*, Book 19, 17.

2. Augustine, Epistle 189.

unaware of the dangers that the military ethos might pose to Christians. He cautioned against "vicious and perverse desire" and condemned such things as the "cruelty of revenge," and "lust of domination," instead urging soldiers, as agents of God's will to be chaste and disciplined, intent only on serving peace.[3]

In the context of his world, Augustine answered the question "When is war justifiable?" by pointing to the value of a well-knit social order in which people may procure the necessities of life. He supported military defense, and the military profession which made such defense possible, while prescribing an almost ascetic way of life for those under arms. Although it would be almost 700 years before scholastic theologians retrieved and appropriated just-war thought as a coherent and continuous tradition in the West, Augustine is credited with suggesting the first three conditions of justifiable war: *just cause, honorable intention,* and *legitimate authority.*

In Chapter Six we will consider whether Augustine's justification of war amounted to a reversal of earlier Christian attitudes toward war. But the very fact that Augustine offered a carefully qualified justification should remind us of the strong presumption against war in the Christian tradition. The theory is intended to be restrictive, combining a "general attitude of opposition to violence and bloodshed with a limited justification of the use of violence by Christians."[4]

Eight conditions have come to comprise the just-war tradition. The first six criteria function to determine *when resort to war is justifiable* and are known as the *jus ad bellum* criteria:

1. just cause;

2. legitimate authority to declare and prosecute war;

3. a right intention;

4. prior attempts to resolve conflict nonmilitarily;

---

3. St. Augustine, *Against Faustus*, 22:74.

4. James Johnson, *The Quest for Peace* (Princeton, NJ: Princeton University Press, 1987), 51.

5. a calculus that greater good than harm will be expected to result;

6. strong prospect that war will produce peace.

Two additional criteria dictate *how war is to be justly conducted* (*jus in bello*):

7. noncombatants may not be directly attacked;

8. combatants may not be subjected to greater harm than is necessary to achieve military victory.

The just-war conditions became the subject of public discussion in the fall and spring of 1990-91 as world leaders considered what to do about Iraq's invasion of Kuwait. Many Catholic and Protestant church leaders opposed the use of military force to compel Iraq's withdrawal. They made their case on just-war grounds but they did not prevail. The advocates of war appealed to these same grounds, invoking just-war criteria to legitimate a short but cruel war against Iraq. In this and the next three chapters we will explore (1) how just-war theory is designed to exert a restraining influence on warmaking and (2) how well it functioned during the Gulf crisis. The reader is asked to suspend disbelief, at least for the time being, if he or she doubts that any theory of restraint is of any practical value in restraining the use of military force. The just-war tradition highlights several salient moral features of international conflict and the use of force to assist in making responsible moral judgments.

1. Just Cause: A Contemporary Case Study

Iraq invaded, occupied and annexed Kuwait on August 2, 1990. Occupying Iraqi soldiers killed, tortured, and sexually abused Kuwaitis and plundered their property. Other nations quickly denounced Iraq's aggression. U.S. President George Bush accused Iraq of "naked aggression" and characterized Saddam Hussein as "another Hitler."

The demand for Iraq's immediate withdrawal was accompanied by swift action. The U.S. froze all Iraqi assets held in U.S. banks, instantly compounding Iraq's economic crisis. Aided by British Prime Minister Margaret Thatcher, Bush enlisted the support of the European Economic Community and NATO to impose trade sanctions and an oil embargo on Iraq. On August 6, the U.N. endorsed a world-wide trade embargo on Iraq. When rumors of Iraqi troop movements along the Saudi Arabian border surfaced on August 7, Bush dispatched 15,000 U.S. troops "to assist the Saudi Arabian government in the defense of its homeland." The next day, the U.S. Defense Department announced that 50,000 U.S. troops would be deployed to Saudi Arabia. On August 9, that number was increased to 100,000, and the White House announced that a coalition of nations had been formed to carry out U.N. resolutions against Iraq. The President's decisive actions — which had surprised even his closest advisors — culminated five months later in an intense air-war against Iraq.

What was this large military response intended to accomplish? President Bush stated five objectives for the deployment of troops to the Gulf:

1. to force Iraq's withdrawal from Kuwait;

2. to restore the government of Kuwait;

3. to protect Saudi Arabia;

4. to restore the stability of the Gulf region;

5. to protect U.S. citizens in the Middle East.

Before long, the Administration articulated an equal number of *additional* objectives:

6. to protect U.S. vital interests;

7. to oust Saddam Hussein;

8. to reduce Iraq's military capability;

9. to destroy Iraq's chemical and (potential) nuclear threat;

10. to establish a "new world order."

While there was widespread agreement that something must be done to reverse Iraq's aggression, what was disconcerting was the lengthy list of "necessary" objectives in addition to freeing Kuwait. Without the benefit of public discussion, all of these objectives were suddenly unfurled under the banner of "just cause."

As the crisis unfolded, President Bush expressed full confidence that the escalating actions against Iraq were justified. On the eve of the war, he declared: "Our cause could not be more noble for it is right, moral, and just."[5] *The New Republic* quoted the President as saying, "I've reconciled all the moral issues. It's white versus black, good versus evil."[6]

Although religious leaders both in the U.S. and abroad denounced Iraq's aggression, for the most part they had deep reservations about resorting to war against Iraq. One of their reservations was over the inflated number of objectives that military action would need to accomplish. U.S. Archbishop Roger Mahoney of Los Angeles urged the President to "clarify [U.S. policy's] precise objectives" and challenged the President to "demonstrate that it (the objectives) can only be achieved through the use of force."[7] Likewise, Archbishop John Roach told the Senate Foreign Relations Committee that the "difficult question . . . was not whether Iraq's action should be opposed, but how best to do it."[8] Roach was especially critical of the emerging objectives and the relatively little public discussion of them. He warned the Senators that the nation could "find itself fighting a war without clarity of purpose, public and political consensus, or adequate moral justification."[9] Citing six of the Bush administration's objectives (defending the Saudis, liberating the Kuwaitis, liberating hostages held by Iraq, stabilizing the Mideast, guaranteeing access to oil, and

---

5. *Origins* 35, 572.

6. *The New Republic* (February 25, 1994).

7. *Origins*, Vol 20, 251.

8. *Origins*, Vol 20, 458.

9. *Origins*, Vol 20, 459.

preventing Iraq's bid for nuclear capability), Roach observed that the longer the list the more difficult it would be to achieve "clarity of purpose or success." Roach cautioned that the logic of such a long list of objectives meant that achieving all of them would become the minimally acceptable outcome and that achieving anything less would be viewed as a defeat. The effect, he concluded, would be to view the use of force as absolutely necessary in order to avoid defeat.

The objections Mahoney and Roach raised demonstrate how just cause is intended to limit the resort to war. Objectives for undertaking military action must be carefully articulated and defended by policy-makers since this sort of government undertaking, like no other, requires citizens to kill and to die.

It is important to recognize that moralists have tried to limit the causes for which war is justifiable. In the sixteenth century Spanish theologian Francisco de Vittoria denied that nations could claim religious ground for their causes against other peoples; his intent was to delegitimate wars in defense of religion. Vittoria's restrictive interpretation of just cause discouraged elevating secular causes into divine ones. Crusades and "holy wars" were not, in his view, just-wars.

In the seventeenth century, the Dutch Protestant Hugh Grotius qualified just cause in another way. Grotius asserted that the claims of *all parties* in international disputes were simultaneously both just and unjust. Grotius did not deny the possibility that one nation's claim to justice might be sufficiently stronger than another's to justify its use of force. But he sought to emphasize that just-war analysis demanded attending to several criteria and did not turn only on the issue of just cause. And justness of cause was very rarely black and white but a matter of shades of grey. The echo of Grotius can be heard in the Catholic Bishops' 1983 pastoral letter, when the Bishops ask how it is to be determined that one nation is "sufficiently 'right' in a dispute . . . to override the presumption against war." Recalling Grotius, they write:

The category of comparative justice is designed to emphasize the presumption against war which stands at the beginning of just war teaching. In a world of sovereign states recognizing neither a common moral authority nor a central political authority, comparative justice stresses that no nation should act on the basis that it has "absolute justice" on its side. Every party of a conflict should acknowledge the limits of its "just cause" and the consequent requirement to use *only* limited means in pursuit of its objectives. Far from legitimizing a crusade mentality, comparative justice is designed to relativize absolute claims and restrain the use of force even in a "justified" conflict.[10]

The notion of "comparative justice" is intended to encourage the resolution of international disputes without recourse to war. When nations can acknowledge that justice and injustice are present to some degree in each other's claims, they are more likely to make concessions and accommodations to one another. Recognizing at least the partial legitimacy of the adversary's claims is the first step in the process of mediating disputes rather than resorting to war. When nations claim that "absolute justice" is on their side, conflicts take on a dangerous dualism: "we are good, they are evil"; "we are light, they are darkness." Such dualism fosters a crusade mentality blinding nations to their own injustices. Nations embarked upon a crusade lose the capacity for critical deliberation about the ends they hope to achieve and the means by which they might achieve them. Believing their cause alone is just, they are easily tempted to permit anything to further it. Disputing nations that recognize the limits of their justice claims may be more moderate in the objectives they seek. What both Grotius and the U.S. Catholic Bishops recognized is the greater difficulty of arbitrating disputes between nations than within a nation. Consensus about the common good and what constitutes just so-

---

10. National Conference of Catholic Bishops, *The Challenge of Peace: God's Promise and Our Response*, (Washington, DC: Catholic Conference, 1983), para.92-93.

cial, political, and economic arrangements is more likely to be present *within* a nation with a common heritage and shared resources than *between* nations with different histories and cultural values.

In this century as well, we see evidence of further attempts to qualify the condition of just cause more restrictively. Pope Pius XII taught often about the limited justification for the use of force and specified very narrowly the causes for which war may be justly undertaken. Pius held that war was permissible only for the purpose of defending peoples against injustices in the process of occurring. Wars to remedy injustice already committed, wars to punish nations for past injustices, wars to preempt nations who might commit future injustices, and wars of aggression are all disqualified on his interpretation of just cause grounds.

When the U.S. bishops evaluated the litany of "just causes" for military action against Iraq in the fall of 1990, they were right to object to the expansiveness and vagueness of the list that could lead to an escalation of the means necessary to achieve all of them. They were right to take a more restrictive approach recognizing the injustice that had been perpetrated against Kuwait but placing limits on the appropriate response to it. Indeed, "just cause" is susceptible to becoming an inflammatory and inflationary war cry with which to embark on a crusade — in direct contrast to its original intention as a limiting condition for resorting to war.

The Vatican, too, was skeptical of the multiple objectives. The editors of *La Civiltà Cattolica*, a Roman journal reviewed by the Vatican Secretariat of State before publication, reflected Pius XII's restrictive interpretation of just cause and questioned the justification of any of the objectives except for the defense of Kuwait. They wrote: "In reality, war today — except in the case of defending oneself from a grave aggression underway — is morally unacceptable, whatever reasons given for its justification."[11]

---

11. *La Civiltà Cattolica*, Vol 19 (November 17, 1990).

Both the U.S. bishops and *La Civiltà Cattolica* underscored the limiting intent of the just-war principles, beginning with the careful scrutiny of objectives — objectives to be pursued by nonmilitary means unless and/or until other conditions are present for justifiable resort to armed conflict.

What might have contributed to a negotiated settlement of the Gulf crisis would have been a greater appreciation of the "comparative justice" issues in the Middle East. A brief history lesson on colonialism along the following lines might have helped. In the view of many Iraqis, Iraq had been victimized by its Arab neighbors, by Israel, and by the West. Thus, Hussein and many other Iraqis viewed the invasion of Kuwait as an attempt to redress violations of Iraqi economic and political rights that had been occurring for over seven decades. As one British historian acknowledged, British and French domination of the Middle East after World War I "created a situation where people felt they had been wronged." The case can be made that the Gulf crisis of 1990 began in 1922. In that year, Britain, acting under a League of Nations Mandate, assumed control of Iraqi resources and politics while also arbitrarily creating the borders between Iraq, Saudi Arabia, and Kuwait. Britain ruled Iraq until 1932 when it installed a royal family favorable to British interests. That family maintained power until a coup in 1958.

To Hussein, the emirates of the Gulf and their oil-rich sheiks were pawns of Western interests who symbolized the failure of wealthy Arabs to care for the poor Arab masses. Saddam Hussein styled himself as capable of forging pan-Arab unity. He viewed Iran, the oil-rich sheiks, and Israel as hostile to that unity. While it may well be that Hussein cared little for the plight of the stateless Palestinians, he nonetheless perceived Israel as a military threat. Indeed, in 1981, in direct violation of Iraqi sovereignty and without Western protest, Israel had bombed Iraq's nuclear reactor outside of Baghdad. In 1989, a weapons expert under contract with Hussein's government had been assassinated by Israeli security agents.

Iraq's eight-year war with Iran had, by 1989, brought Iraq to the brink of economic collapse. Believing that Iraq had borne the disproportionate burden of containing Iran's militant Islamic fundamentalism (a cause which the U.S. had endorsed), Hussein demanded economic assistance from other Arab countries. He insisted upon a moratorium on the debts Iraq had incurred during the war, new credit, and restrictions on oil production in order to help boost Iraqi oil revenues. In February 1990, Arab states refused both Hussein's request for more credit and relaxation on repayment of Iraq's $80 billion war debt. In addition, OPEC nations rejected his request to cut oil production.

The immediate source of Iraq's sense of victimization was its border with the Emirate of Kuwait, which had been disputed since it was first drawn in 1922. Not only had Kuwait rejected Hussein's February 1990 plea to reduce oil production, it actually *increased* its oil production. On July 16, Iraqi Foreign Minister Asiz accused Kuwait of making economic war on Iraq by its theft of oil from the Rumaila oil fields. Iraq demanded $2.4 billion in compensation from Kuwait. This demand was rejected. From Hussein's point of view, the issue that precipitated his invasion of Kuwait was nothing less than Iraq's rightful claims. This was the context for Hussein's rash remedy on August 2. The injustice which caught the world's attention eclipsed the long series of prior injustices that had precipitated it.

But without this historical perspective, Hussein's invasion appeared to be an unprovoked attack by a dangerous and unpredictable dictator who was not amenable to reason.

Indeed, Hussein was dangerous, not only because he was unreasonable but because the U.S. government and private arms dealers had been supplying him with military hardware for a decade.[12] Throughout the fall of 1990, the focus remained

---

12. After the war, it was learned that Western governments, chief among them the U.S., had been delivering to Iraq the latest in high-tech military equipment up until the invasion of Kuwait. In addition to receiving military aid, Hussein was among the most valued customers of private arms dealers in Europe and the United States.

on Iraq's (and specifically Hussein's) criminal behavior. As condemnations and threats against Iraq escalated alongside the list of objectives of military action, many Americans suspected that their government was irrevocably intent on war.

Bush's appeal to several just causes would not have been endorsed by Vittoria, Grotius, and Pius XII. What was essential but missing was public discussion about the particular military objectives and their justification. Suspicions arose that events were proceeding along a predetermined course. The editors of the *New York Times* challenged President Bush to explain just how Iraq's actions posed a threat to our "vital interests," our way of life, and our freedom, as he claimed. While Bush had avoided mentioning oil, others in the Administration had linked oil with U.S. vital interests. Indeed, oil appeared to be the link between Saudi Arabia's security and the western standard of living. Prescinding from the questions of whether the protection of U.S. oil interests was an objective in the showdown against Hussein and, even more critically, of whether it was a justifiable objective, there is little doubt that it functioned as a powerful, unstated objective behind operations Desert Shield and Desert Storm.

One reality check on the list of objectives in the Gulf is to consider whether the urgency with which they were invoked had validity. Did deploying U.S. troops to the Gulf, for example, prevent an Iraqi invasion of Saudi Arabia? In fact, Iraq showed no signs of having an appetite for that neighbor and, ironically, the Saudis soon grew apprehensive about the presence of U.S. forces. This objective, which had served to rationalize the deployment of over 100,000 troops (and over 400,000 after U.S. congressional elections in November), gradually lost its force. Had Iraq ever intended to invade Saudi Arabia or was it actually deterred from doing so by the show of forces amassed against it? Iraq had neither a historic border dispute with Saudi Arabia nor a current dispute with it over oil production quotas. In addition, the U.S. had no intelligence predictions of an Iraqi invasion of Saudi Arabia as it had in 1989 prior to Iraq's invasion of Kuwait. In September, Hussein eliminated an additional objective by releasing all Americans being held in Iraq. The "new world order" Bush envisioned received no careful articulation and found no public support. Likewise, the wisdom of eliminating Hussein, the appropriate means of reducing of Iraq's military power and stabilizing the Gulf Region received scant public discussion. Only the liberation of Kuwait remained a compelling cause. Yet the danger in such an expansive list of objectives, vaguely linked to one another, was its inflamatory effect. So many objectives broadened the grounds for war and, when war came, inflated its aims.

2. War Against Iraq: By Whose Authority?

Who is supposed to be applying the several just-war criteria? The question is always a crucial one, and particularly so in a constitutional democracy such as ours. The earliest just-war thinkers could not have imagined the awesome military power at the command of the "commander-in-chief." Nor could they have they envisioned the delicate balance of powers established to prevent its reckless use. The issue of authority arose with other concerns.

In the sixth century the Roman Empire disintegrated and resulted in a dispersal of political power and the rise of regional powers. Political tensions developed — similar to the tensions between the various ethnic republics that have become autonomous since the breakup of the Soviet Union. The church responded to the proliferation of centers of power and the frequency of warmaking by attempting to place "legitimate authority" with only the largest political units.

If giving only larger political entities the authority to wage war helped to limit the outbreak of war in the sixth century, it certainly did little to discourage warfare from keeping pace with the political consolidations that culminated in the emergence of "nation-states" in the sixteenth century. The monarchs of these states poured ever-vaster amounts of national wealth into armies and navies. Military campaigns were monarchs' preoccupation. The right to make war belonged to the sovereign — and later, when kings were deposed, became the uncontested prerogative of the nation's will. Warmaking and national sovereignty became synonymous. Political theorist Hannah Arendt has argued that the framers of the U.S. Constitution, by requiring foreign treaties to be "part and parcel of the law of the land," denied the President the sovereignty exercised by European monarchs.[13] The requirement of Congressional approval intends that military policies be given the same scrutiny as all other executive policies.

Since the dawn of the modern period, appeals have been heard for the creation of a world authority to resolve disputes between nations. But the movement toward internationalism has made most progress in the twentieth century. Pope Pius XII labored diligently to promote the vision of an international community within which individual nations would recognize their common bond. He promoted an international order in which warmaking would give way to negotiation allowing "the force of reason [to] prevail over the violence of arms."[14] Pius appealed for the imposition of limits on the power of individual states, writing:

> Now no one can fail to see how the claim to absolute autonomy for the State . . . leaves the stability of international relations at the mercy of the will of rulers, while it destroys the possibility of true union and fruitful collaboration directed to the general good.[15]

The framers of the U.S. Constitution took seriously Lord Acton's dictum that "power corrupts and absolute power corrupts absolutely" when they established checks and balances on the use of military power. The president commands the forces; Congress must authorize funds for military action. In all, the framers wanted to give the electorate greater influence over the use of military power. If this was the theoretical intent, in practice the executive and legislative branches perenni-

---

13. Hannah Arendt, "On Violence," in *Crisis in the Republic* (New York: Harcourt Brace Jovanovich, Inc., 1969).

14. Pius XII, Address, *Un'ora grave*, 24 August 1939.

15. Pius XII, Encyclical, *Summi Pontificatus*, 20 October 1939.

ally struggle over the issue of who is to make the call about war. The struggle between president and Congress intensified dramatically as the Vietnam War deepened, culminating in the passage of legislation (the War Powers Act of 1973) whereby Congress attempted to reassert its power and prevent future "presidential wars."

From the beginning of the Gulf conflict, the Administration had managed U.S. involvement with minimal consultation of Congress. In October 1990, Secretary of State Baker had testified before the Senate Foreign Relations Committee that the sanctions should be given time to work. But the day after the November congressional elections, the country was taken by surprise as the White House announced the doubling of troop levels in the Gulf. President Bush waited until a U.S. military force of 400,000 was assembled in the Gulf and on full alert and until the deadline he had imposed on Iraq was two days away before he sought congressional approval.

In January 1991, as the deadline approached for Iraq to withdraw from Kuwait, the Bush Administration claimed that the president did not need congressional approval but had executive authority to organize the coalition and engage U.S. forces. Despite this claim, Bush's supporters urged him to seek congressional authorization in order to avoid a potential constitutional showdown. On January 12 and 13, the Senate and House debated the issue and voted by slim margins (52-47 and 250-183) to support the President.[16]

With one day of debate and little more than a split vote, Operation Desert Storm began on January 17. Its timetable and the momentum that the Administration had orchestrated raised the question whether the President would have acted against Iraq without the consent of Congress. The Gulf War was clearly a "presidential war." Acting quickly and unilaterally, the President managed events in such a way that his decision

---

16. See Alan Geyer and Barbara Green, *Lines in the Sand: Justice and the Gulf War* (Louisville: Westminster/John Knox Press, 1991), p. 125. They argue that some members of Congress voted for the resolution under the assumption that their vote would avert war.

to use military force against Iraq met no successful challenge or delay.

The power to wage war has tremendous consequences. John Courtney Murray, theologian and statesman, wrote that the condition of legitimate authority

> insists, first, that military decisions are a species of political decisions, and second, that political decisions must be viewed, not simply in the perspectives of politics as an exercise in power, but of morality and theology in some valid sense. If military and political decisions are not so viewed, the result is the degradation of those who make them and the destruction of the human community.[17]

Murray recognized that, in a democracy, lively public discourse on policy issues offered the best hope for a moral politics. He asserted that war is not something primarily for the politicians and generals to decide, but that it is a moral matter about which "the People shall judge."[18] Murray insisted this was the responsibility of citizens and lamented over its general neglect:

> This is their responsibility, to be discharged before the shooting starts, by an active concern with the moral direction of national policy. My impression is that this duty in social morality is being badly neglected in America at the moment.[19]

That "the people shall judge" is a reminder of the role of a well-informed public opinion exerting influence on the decisions of elected leadership. This is not to suggest that majority rule insures a moral politics, but rather to point out the danger of the absence of public debate in critical decisions about war.

The movement toward international efforts to regulate the conduct of nations that has marked this century was also evi-

---

17. John Courtney Murray, "War and Conscience" in *A Conflict of Loyalties*, James Finn, ed. (New York: Pegasus, 1968), 21.

18. Murray, *We Hold These Truths* (New York: Sheed and Ward, 1960), 257.

19. Murray, ibid.

dent in the Gulf conflict. Within days of Iraq's invasion of Kuwait the U.N. Security Council — no longer the scene of a standoff between superpowers — acted decisively, passing a series of 12 resolutions against Iraq. The first of them, U.N. Resolution 660, was passed the day of Iraq's invasion, and called for the immediate and unconditional withdrawal of Iraqi forces from Kuwait. On August 6, Resolution 661 imposed economic sanctions on Iraq.

President Bush attempted to legitimate his action by claiming that the Coalition he had established was acting on behalf of the United Nations. However, he was not acting at the behest of the U.N. in organizing a coalition against Iraq. Nor was the military force deployed to the Gulf a U.N. peacekeeping operation. Instead, it was predominantly a U.S. military operation joined by small numbers of British, French, Italian, Saudi, and Egyptian forces. The authority under which these forces was assembled was that of the President of the United States with support from several other nations. On August 19, 1990, the *New York Times* reported that Bush and his closest advisers had made "pivotal decisions" regarding how they would respond to Iraq. Ironically, that same day Senator Joseph Biden called for "extensive debate" on the commitment of U.S. troops to the region. It appeared to be only a matter of time: and when U.N. Resolution 678 was passed by the Security Council in November, authorizing "all necessary means" to uphold and implement Resolution 660 if Iraq did not comply by January 15, the stage was set for war. Alan Dowty assessed Resolution 678 in this way:

> When the U.S. government succeeded in late November in getting the Security Council to adopt a deadline for Iraqi compliance, it was clear there would be no peaceful retreat. . . . There is evidence that Bush himself, at least, did initially expect the deadline to do the trick, and if so it is a glaring case of the lack of understanding of the Arab world. But it was not a grievous error from the Administration's standpoint, since it was just as willing to go to war as to win without war.[20]

Despite several diplomatic initiatives proposed by France and the Soviet Union, prospects of avoiding war dimmed quickly.[21] As Dowty notes, "the locus of decision on when and how to launch military action against Iraq passed from the Security Council to the White House in an inexplicable and almost uncontested fashion."[22] Furthermore, the White House was concerned that the coalition would not hold up if its forces did not move quickly against Iraq. Despite the U.N. Resolutions, the Gulf war was largely a U.S. war with only the appearance of U.N. direction. Secretary General Javier Perez de Quayar publicly stated that the operation was *not* under U.N. auspices. U.N. peacekeeping forces were sent to Kuwait only after the war was over.

The tension between executive and legislative branches of U.S. government are mirrored in the tension between international authority and the unilateral prerogatives of nations. Progress toward greater international cooperation is reflected in developments of international law and organization. The U.N. offers the potential for collective action to mediate international disputes, defuse conflicts, and reestablish political and economic order. Under the terms of the U.N. Charter, the Security Council has the authority to take diplomatic, economic, and military measures to protect nations against aggression. Yet nations may assert claims of national sovereignty to block efforts of the U.N. to act against widespread human rights violations. Hannah Arendt is not hopeful that genuine international authority can be established "so long as national independence, namely freedom from foreign rule, and the sovereignty of the state, namely, the claim to unchecked and unlimited power in foreign affairs, are identified."[23] Indeed, in its 45-year existence (the Cold War era) the Security Council was

---

20. Dowty, 31.

21. See, "At The Brink" *Maclean's* Vol. 104 No. 4 (January 14, 1991) and *The Nation* Vol. 252 No. 6 (February 18, 1991).

22. Dowty, 30.

23. Arendt, 107.

able to take enforcement action only three times: sending military assistance to South Korea, imposing an arms embargo on South Africa, and boycotting Southern Rhodesia.[24] In 1990, the end of the Superpower standoff provided an opportune moment to respond to Iraq's invasion of Kuwait in a genuinely international effort.

3. Could War Have Been Prevented?

St. Augustine counselled those who wage war to do so with "right intention." He warned against dishonorable motives and hidden agendas under the guise of seeking justice. Clearly, Iraq's aggression was patently unjust and the President's announced intention to remedy that injustice cannot be questioned. But what must be asked is whether other motives and agendas were creating a momentum for war throughout the fall of 1990 that made a negotiated settlement of the crisis impossible.

The question of motives must be raised because of the way in which the conflict was handled from the moment Iraq attacked Kuwait. From that point on a vigorous "war of words" was undertaken against Hussein. Indeed, the propaganda against Iraq was intense. The Kuwaitis had hired a Washington public relations firm to lobby Congress on their behalf. The most dramatic moment in the public relations campaign occurred when the daughter of Kuwait's ambassador to the U.S. testified to the Senate Foreign Relations Committee that Iraqi occupiers had removed Kuwaiti newborns from their incubators in a hospital nursery in Kuwait City and left them to die, a claim that the hospital staff denied after the war. A Washington policy analysis group charged that Hussein had begun "a war of resources," by which he intended to control the region's oil resources. But the analysis was silent regarding the bitter dispute over war debts, oil production quotas, and ownership of the Rumaila oil fields which Hussein believed

---

24. Dowty, 13.

represented a war against Iraq's vital interests. Such propaganda obscured the claims and counterclaims that had been made in the region for almost seven decades, effectively denying that the rationale for Iraqi annexation of Kuwait had a history. Although discussion of justice issues in the Gulf region prior to Iraq's unjust seizure of Kuwait is not to plead Iraqi innocence or to suggest that Iraq's action should have been allowed to stand, not to discuss such issues may have resulted in only a short-term solution to the Kuwaiti crisis and dimmed prospects for a lasting peace.

The days immediately after the beginning of the crisis were marked by increasing threats against Hussein, who was characterized as "another Hitler." On August 11 President Bush urged the Iraqi people to "do something about Saddam Hussein." Was the intent really to get Hussein to remove his forces from Kuwait or to create a standoff, and precipitate a war to remove him?

The function of the just-war tradition is to forestall rushing headlong into military confrontations. What other avenues might have been traveled to settle the dispute short of the use of force? Instead of waging a propaganda war against Hussein what might have been done in the fall of 1990 to solve the crisis?

In the next chapter we will consider other ways in which Iraq's aggression might have been checked. Could the liberation of Kuwait have been accomplished by nonmilitary or limited military action rather than by wholesale destruction of Iraq's major cities and infrastructure and the death of thousands of its people?

Questions for Reflection

1. How would you assess Hussein's claim that Kuwait was guilty of economic aggression against Iraq? Do you think there are instances in which economic and military aggression are comparable injustices?

2. While John Courtney Murray that in a democracy faced with the prospect of war, the "people shall judge." Identify some of the factors in the nature of American politics and government that prevent the people from judging. How would it be possible for citizens to reassert their influence? How would we establish the necessary conditions for genuine public debate?

3. The role of the media is to provide citizens with the information needed to make critical political and moral judgments. From your recollection of the coverage of the Gulf crisis and war, how would assess the way the news media functioned? What kind of improvements would you suggest?

4. Do you think the U.S. government has an adequate system of checks and balances to prevent abuse of military power. If not, what do you think can be done to prevent future "presidential wars"?

5. Do you see the United Nations playing a more central role in mediating international and intra-national disputes. What features should an effective international peacekeeping mechanism have?

CHAPTER THREE

When Is War Justified? The Criteria of Proportionality, Success, and Last Resort

Introduction

We have emphasized that Christianity maintains a strong presumption against war. Here we will examine three criteria that are intended to function as additional restraints against warmaking in the just-war tradition. The criteria of last resort, proportionality, and probability of success were developed in the late Middle Ages by churchmen and jurists. While the issues of just cause, rightness of intention, and legitimacy of authority may sometimes be controversial, these three criteria we will discuss all involve predicting future outcomes which, because of limited knowledge, can be no more than rough estimations. As difficult as predicting future eventualities and weighing future outcomes is, these just-war conditions counsel prudence and foresight. We must try to see down the road, to see where the course of action we commence today may be expected to deliver us tomorrow. This chapter will focus on these three criteria and observe how they were applied — or not applied — to the Gulf conflict.

1. Last Resort

The criterion of last resort requires that other means of resolving conflict be pursued and given time to work before resorting to the use of military force. This condition is a reminder that resorting to force amounts to crossing a critical threshold.[1] It does not specify what other means must be tried or when non-military approaches have been exhausted. What it does demand is that other means must be pursued to resolve international conflicts.

Four months after Iraq occupied Kuwait, the U.S. government expressed the conviction that Hussein could be forced to give up Kuwait only by military means. The Administration offered a two-fold argument for the virtual necessity of a military operation against Iraq. First, Saddam Hussein had refused all diplomatic initiatives. Second, economic sanctions could not be expected to work because sanctions, like diplomacy, could only succeed when dealing with a rational opponent, which Hussein was not. Hussein's continued occupation and victimization of Kuwait argued against postponing action against him. If anything, it was time to send a message to other petty tyrants: behave like Hussein and we will crush you. On November 29, 1990 the U.N. Security Council passed resolution 678, authorizing member states "to use all necessary means" to restore Kuwait's sovereignty unless Iraq withdrew its forces from Kuwait by January 15, 1991.

Let us consider the negotiations and economic sanctions which the Bush Administration declared to have failed and which thereby warranted a military option. Beginning on August 2, 1990, Iraq was presented with a number of demands, all having to do with the restoration of Kuwait's freedom. Ensuing diplomatic efforts to gain Iraq's compliance were unsuccessful and the stalemate quickly became a showdown.

---

1. In a similar way, those who advocated in the nineteenth century that nations must make formal declarations of war were putting emphasis on that threshold, hoping that nations would offer one another a "last chance" to avoid crossing it.

What about the diplomatic efforts that were made to reverse Iraq's aggression? Political scientist Alan Dowty offered a distinction between two models of international conflict resolution: the negotiation and the enforcement model.[2] In the negotiation model the parties in a conflict work toward compromises on the substantive issues involved. The enforcement model involves face-saving concessions to a nation guilty of violating international laws but involves no substantive negotiations. President Bush and the rest of the international community pursued the enforcement model by making it clear from the start that Iraq's exit from Kuwait was nonnegotiable, a stance with which Dowty agrees. The nearly unanimous condemnation of Iraq underscored lack of support within the Coalition for a negotiation process that would yield to Iraq's claims on Kuwait.[3]

Dowty does not argue that face-saving concessions alone would have been enough to persuade Hussein to leave Kuwait immediately. But he does note that the nations arrayed against Iraq were in a much stronger position to force Iraq's compliance than Iraq was to resist. Dowty points to Chapter Seven of the U.N. Charter, which enumerates the means of achieving nonvoluntary compliance of offending nations, ranging from diplomatic and economic sanctions to the use of military force. This was only the third time in its history that the U.N. had invoked Chapter Seven and the first time since the end of the Cold War. The confrontation with Iraq, he writes, was an auspicious opportunity to achieve "the first enforcement action by the Security Council carried out according to the original vision" of effective U.N. enforcement against an international violator. The forces arrayed against Iraq suggested that enforcement could be achieved "at a reasonable cost and without war."[4] Instead, a verbal barrage against Hussein worked to in-

---

2. Alan Dowty, "The Gulf War: A View From No Man's Land," 10ff.

3. Dowty also observes that the call for further diplomatic efforts was weakened by the vagueness of appeals to "negotiate" a settlement. In addition, some seemed to have played into Hussein's hands by allowing him to link the question of Kuwait to the plight of the Palestinians.

sure that Hussein would not give up Kuwait. The President of the United States said publicly of Hussein: "We'll kick his ass."

Dowty was joined by many others who argued that enforcement, supported by economic sanctions, would have worked. The economic sanctions imposed against Iraq on August 6, forbade all trade with Iraq, except for the import of medical supplies and foodstuffs in "humanitarian circumstances," and froze all Iraqi assets abroad. Secretary of State James Baker testified to Congress in early September and mid-October, 1990, that economic sanctions should be given time to work. Yet on November 8, a massive troop build-up was announced, signaling the Administration's impatience with that approach. Would they have worked? The very motives which had led Hussein to invade Kuwait underscore how economically weakened Iraq already was. Its monetary reserves were low due to the war with Iran, and it was highly dependent on foreign goods in exchange for oil.[5] Iraq's use of the sea was blocked by U.N. resolution 665 (August 25, 1990). It was surrounded by now-hostile neighbors. It no longer had the patronage of the Soviet Union, one of several foreign sources of military resupply upon which its military strength depended.

Dowty reports that the economic sanctions imposed on Iraq were the most extensive ever adopted by the U.N. Furthermore, he writes,

> A study of one hundred and fifteen economic sanction cases since World War I, carried out by the Institute for International Economics, found that the estimated impact of the sanctions against Iraq was *twenty times* greater than the average impact of previous *successful* applications of sanctions (one-third of the total), and three times as great as the previous highest impact cases. Based on past patterns, the study projected the probability of success at 100 percent, and estimated that the time required would be about one year. Similar conclusions were suggested by CIA Director William

---

4. Dowty, 15-16.

5. Dowty, 13.

Webster, in December testimony before Congress: "Probably only energy-related and some military industries will still be functioning by next spring."[6]

The study Dowty reports predicted that, within one year, economic sanctions would cost Iraq 48% of its GNP.

Economic sanctions create shortages which weaken military capability and impose hardships on civilians. In addition to the question of efficiency is the issue of the morality of economic sanctions. Imposing economic sanctions is not a morally neutral act. Sanctions hurt the civilian population. The most vulnerable sectors of the population suffer deprivations first while the political and military establishments are the last to feel the effects. The argument has been made that economic sanctions are a form of violence against civilians. Like bombing in urban areas, it is said, sanctions intend to create civilian resentment and political havoc. Regarding Iraq, it was argued that the precision bombing in urban areas was morally preferable to sanctions because the bombing was less harmful to the overall civilian population than prolonged sanctions would have been. Ethicist James Johnson compared sanctions to the medieval practice of laying siege to a city, in effect, taking the whole population hostage.[7]

The argument that sanctions may be more objectionable than warfare is a weak one. The degree of harm resulting from economic sanctions and from destruction of social infrastructure of a society are considerably different. Sanctions deprive a population by a process of attrition and allow it time to find ways of making do with less: the system still works and food and medicine are still available. When the sanctions are lifted, normal operations can be restored relatively quickly. But destruction of infrastructure severs vital services, food supply channels, and the means of emergency medical care. Restoring normal life requires months and even years (as U.N. missions

---

6. Dowty, 16. The sanctions study was reported in the *New York Times*, January 14, 1991. Webster's testimony was reported in the *New York Times*, Dec. 6, 1990.

7. James Johnson, "The Just-War Tradition and The American Military."

to Iraq after the war documented). As we will see in more detail in the next chapter, the coalition's targeting within Iraq was extensive, going well beyond targets of direct military value. In addition, 93% of the bombs dropped on Iraq were not precision bombs. Their use resulted in extensive civilian deaths, injuries, and damage. The air war against civilians did more harm to civilians than a year of sanctions could possibly have done.

A U.S. poll taken on January 10th showed that 45% of Americans favored continued sanctions and 41% favored military action. But President Bush was impatient and "couldn't wait too long without losing the Coalition," as Langan noted.[8] The January 15th deadline undercut the sanctions and set the stage for a "showdown" between the forces of "good" and "evil." In effect, the deadline helped to precipitate war, casting aside both diplomacy and sanctions.

But questions remained. Short of war, had there been adequate exploration of other possible responses to Iraq's aggression? It is difficult to avoid the conclusion that President Bush, perceiving that the opportunity for the defining moment of his presidency had arrived, disregarded other options in favor of military action. In the end it may not have been a question of the effectiveness of sanctions but the desire for decisive results.

2. Strategic Proportionality

The principle of proportionality requires that the good for which a war is waged may not be outweighed by the harm it will cause. This is the first of two calculations of benefit-harm that just-war reasoning requires. (I refer to the first as "strategic" proportionality since it is concerned with the overall consequences of warfare; the second is referred to as "tactical" proportionality and is a calculus of the amount of harm necessary to defeat enemy forces.) Concern for strategic proportion-

---

8. John Langan, "An Imperfectly Just War," 363.

ality in a contemplated war with Iraq required considering likely costs against likely outcomes. The Coalition had to ask beforehand "which particular weapons will be used, how they will be used, and for what end" — questions, Walzer added, that render the theory "importantly restrictive."[9] Walzer believed that it would be clearly immoral to initiate a war that would claim the lives of hundreds of thousands and risk nuclear destruction for the sake of liberating Kuwait. Rather, military action that observed the condition of strategic proportionality would have been limited to specific, justifiable objectives and been carried out by means designed to incur the least amount of harm possible on Iraqi society.

How did the U.S. intend to prosecute a war against Iraq?

In the Fall of 1990, the U.S. Air Force devised extensive plans for an air offensive against Iraq. The strategy was to smash every major Iraqi city in the "most intensive bombing campaign in history."[10] Besides destroying military targets in Iraq, the offensive destroyed electrical power, water, sewage treatment, and refrigeration facilities, as well as hospital and clinic operations and all civil government and communications systems in every major Iraqi population center. It is remarkable that the civilian death toll, estimated to be between five and thirteen thousand, was not many times higher. We will postpone until the next chapter a discussion of what is perhaps the most critical just-war requirement: sparing civilians. But the impact of war on civilian society is central to thinking about proportionality. Three months after the war ended, the total number of civilians who had died or suffered long-term ill effects of the bombings due to epidemics, food shortages, or lack of medical care was estimated to be as high as 70,000. Proportionality required taking into account the consequences of destroying the material necessities of life in Iraq. The potential harm to the Iraqi infrastructure should have been ac-

---

9. Walzer, 8.

10. *Air Force Magazine*, March, 1991, 16.

knowledged as one of the major "costs" that had to be weighed against the good of liberating Kuwait.

How was the destruction of the social fabric and infrastructure of Iraq related to the objective of liberating Kuwait? Did it in any way serve to reduce Iraqi military and weapon superiority? Was the stability of the Gulf region enhanced by attacking Iraqi urban society? After the war, the only explanation offered was that such destruction was calculated to undermine the power of Saddam Hussein and his Baath party. If so, the strategy failed.

After the war, *La Civiltà Cattolica* charged that the liberation of Kuwait had been achieved at the price of the destruction of Iraq and the deaths of hundreds of thousands of its people. The disproportion was so great, concluded the Roman journal, that the Persian Gulf war could not be considered just. It accused the U.S. of concealing the extent of the war's casualties and destructiveness.[11]

It is never easy to make judgments of proportionality, or to know precisely how much harm to Iraq would have been permissible in order to liberate Kuwait. Still, what was most disturbing about the Gulf War was that so little concern was expressed for the Iraqi population. Why, after six weeks of relentless bombing of Iraqi cities, was there so little organized opposition in the U.S.? No doubt, the answer could be found in the 400,000 U.S. troops deployed to the region and the great U.S. fear of their engagement in a land war against massive Iraqi forces. The air war was tolerated — or applauded — as necessary to prevent the loss of U.S. lives when a ground war began. The insertion of American lives into the calculus made the disproportionate destruction of Iraq "acceptable." After the war, the U.S. public mood was triumphal. The fact of victory eclipsed the costs (in both human and economic terms). President Bush had called Hussein's bluff and had won. Winning had made the risks acceptable. The price was ignored and the harm forgotten — all the more easily because only a hand-

---

11. *La Civiltà Cattolica*, Vol. 20 (July 6, 1991), 3.

ful of American families had suffered losses of loved ones in the war.

Unlike the Gulf War, the Vietnam War had dragged on for years, eventually forcing the nation to confront the issue of loss and of proportionality. During the crisis in the Gulf, frequent references were made to Vietnam. Nobody — least of all, the military — wanted "another Vietnam." In one respect, the outcome of the Gulf War was different: the war was brief and victory decisive. But in another respect, the disproportionate destruction of both Iraqi and Vietnamese societies made them very similar wars. The charge of disproportionate destruction needed to be raised during both wars. In the Gulf War, two questions were never addressed. First, how did the destruction of Iraq's infrastructure and the suffering imposed upon its people contribute to the liberation of Kuwait? Second, how was freedom for Kuwaitis determined to be a good outweighing the harm to which Iraqis were subjected? The issue of proportionality was not effectively considered before, during, or after the Persian Gulf War.

3. The Probability of Success and Prospect of Peace

The intent of weighing the probability of success is not only to discourage embarking on suicidal military adventures. It is also a reminder that warmaking is only justified when it serves the reestablishing of peace. St. Augustine's advice to Boniface "to be a peacemaker even in waging war" may seem illogical. But the kind of peace this condition has in mind is something less than complete international harmony. The "realistic" goal of war, argues James Childress, is the restoration of "the 'normal' state of affairs as quickly and surely as possible."[12] Loftier goals of peace, he warns, are dangerous insofar as they "may engender a brutal and total war."[13] Johnson concurs:

---

12. James Childress, "Just-War Theories," *Theological Studies* Vol. 39, No. 3 (1978), 439.

13. Childress, 439. See also, Paul Ramsey, *The Just War*, 152.

> The use of force may establish the conditions for order, justice, and peace by eliminating the threats posed to them; that is the most realistic definition of "success" in the use of military force. The actual *achievement* of these goals is the broader work of good statecraft, building on the base of established conditions. . . . It is inappropriate to demand that a just use of force achieve ends beyond its means.[14]

Johnson's realism may be well placed. But realism on another count is also required: namely, that use of excessive force may be counterproductive to establishing the preconditions of peace. One cannot ignore the connection between means and ends expressed in the couplet:

> Point not the goal until you plot the course
> For ends and means to man are tangled so
> That different means quite different aims enforce.
> Conceive the means as ends in embryo.[15]

Let us consider peace in the Gulf in these terms. The first objective of the War was to remove Iraq from Kuwait, restore Kuwait's sovereignty, and require Iraq to make reparations for Kuwaiti losses. In Johnson's estimation, forcing Iraq out of Kuwait would be a first step toward "reordering of the relations among the nations of the region," establishing new mutual security arrangements, and settling the Arab-Israeli conflict.[16] But recall two of the war's other objectives: disarming Iraq and driving Saddam Hussein from power. Political experts worried aloud whether crushing Iraq might drastically destablize the Middle East, perhaps allowing fanatics in Iran to gain greater power in the region. Such a shift in the balance of power would not serve the "new world order" that Bush was envisioning.

---

14. Johnson, "The Just War Tradition and the American Military," 28-29.

15. Quoted by Joan Bonderant, *Conquest of Violence: The Gandhian Philosophy of Conflict* (Berkeley: University of California Press, 1967), xiii.

16. Johnson, op cit.

The lack of limited peace objectives became quite clear during the war. By the war's fifth week Iraqi forces were in desperate straits. Indeed, when U.S. forces liberated Kuwait City a few days later Iraqi military occupiers simply fled for their lives. But the U.S. Administration appeared to have no clear idea of what should happen next. Ferocious attacks on Baghdad continued, apparently as an all-out effort to eliminate Hussein. His retreating troops were subjected to merciless air attacks intended to disarm Iraq even further. Defeated in Kuwait, Hussein now turned his troops on the internal threat to his power: Kurdish and Shi'ite ethnic forces in northwestern Iraq whom President Bush had earlier urged to rebel against Hussein. Thousands of Kurds and Shi'ites were killed and thousands more fled into the mountains of northwest Iraq and into Turkey.

While Operation Desert Storm was declared a success, its supporters were disappointed that the internal politics of Iraq had not changed. They argued that coalition forces should invade Iraq as well, "liberating" Baghdad by ousting Hussein and occupying northwest Iraq to protect the Kurdish and Shiite populations from injustices as great as those suffered by Kuwaitis. But this did not happen.

How effectively had Operation Desert Storm eliminated threats to order, justice, and peace in the region? Indeed, Iraqi military power was greatly reduced and under the terms of surrender Iraq was required to submit to arms inspections and to dismantle its nuclear weapon production facilities. But Iraq has since shown little willingness to cooperate. Although economic sanctions had been dismissed a few months earlier as ineffective, they were immediately reimposed on defeated Iraq in order to force compliance and to accomplish what military force had failed to do: oust Saddam Hussein. By 1994, reports from Baghdad indicated that three years of economic sanctions had created a "hyper-inflation" rate of 6,400%. The cost of bread alone was up 20,000% since 1990.[17]

---

17. Reported from Baghdad by Timothy Llewellyn on the BBC's "The World Tonight" (March 26, 1994).

If anything, Iraq's grievances only multiplied since the end of the War. For instance, in the spring of 1992, in compliance with the terms of surrender, a U.N. mapping team was dispatched to determine a fixed border between Iraq and Kuwait. They established a border which gave Kuwait the contested territory that had precipitated Iraq's invasion of Kuwait a year and a half earlier. Iraqis of all political leanings denounced the new borders while political observers in the Middle East conceded that without direct negotiation between Iraq and Kuwait the long-standing border dispute would not be resolved.[18] History repeated itself: seven decades after a British official had drawn arbitrary borders, a new border was fixed, this time with new high-tech mapping instruments but with little prospect of removing this as a source of future conflict.

Saddam Hussein remained in firm control — a fact testified to by the Bush Administration's tripling of the 1992 CIA budget to $40 million to destabilize Iraq.

The underlying issues of the Gulf conflict remain unresolved. There have been no diplomatic breakthroughs. No nonviolent initiatives were proposed. As Dowty observes, those who opposed use of armed force against Iraq "offered no unified, clear, persuasive answer as to how Iraq would be forced from Kuwait by other means" but instead focused upon the issues of U.S. motives in the Gulf and on U.S. complicity in the injustices of the region.[19] Especially critical and missing were any constructive peace initiatives offered by groups within the Middle East. This peacemaking vacuum, notes Dowty, "made life much easier for those who were advocating quick and overwhelming military force."[20] But the question remains whether the use of military force has created the conditions for peace in the region.

---

18. "Milwaukee Journal," (May 10, 1992).

19. Dowty, 27.

20. Ibid.

Questions for Reflection

1. What kind of economic sanctions are most effective against aggressor nations or factions? What is your assessment of the claim that economic sanctions are more cruel to civilians than military actions?

2. In calculating proportionality, should the value of American soldiers count more than that of Iraqi soldiers? Should American lives count more than Iraqi civilians' lives?

3. In what sense did the Gulf War produce greater stability and peace? In what ways did it sow seeds of future discord?

4. In what ways was the Gulf War similar to and different from the Vietnam War?

5. If you were called upon to go to war for your country, would the objectives and goals of the war influence your decision? If so, in what ways would your support for U.S. military objectives be qualified?

6. If you disagreed with resorting to military action, how far would you go and what means would you use to oppose it? What kind of obstacles would you anticipate to trying to express opposition to a war?

CHAPTER FOUR

How Is War To Be Justly Conducted? The Criteria of Civilian Immunity and Proportionality in Battle

Introduction

For centuries the Church has attempted to minimize the destructiveness of war. Between the eleventh and thirteenth centuries churchmen sought to limit the reach and frequency of warmaking. A movement known as the "Peace of God" attempted to protect civilians from the reach of war by exempting religious, women, children, the elderly, farmers, and tradesmen and various categories of property. The "Truce of God" movement forbade warring on various days of the week (Sundays, Fridays, and holy days) and throughout whole periods of the liturgical year. In the twelfth century the church also attempted to ban the crossbow — and no doubt found itself heavily lobbied by princes and arms makers! If war could not be prevented, the Church's hope was to insist at least upon observing certain restraints once war erupted. This led the way to emphasis on two *jus in bello* conditions: the immunity of noncombatants (also referred to as the principle of discrimination) and the proportionality of the means of executing war.

With the development of vastly more destructive war technologies in the nineteenth century, efforts to restrain war have focused especially on the conduct of war. The chemical warfare used in World War I, the bombing of civilians in World War II (particularly the carpet bombing of German cities), and the nuclear bombs detonated over Hiroshima and Nagasaki, have led to international efforts to protect civilians and to prohibit the use of weapons of mass destruction. As the potential for war's destructiveness has increased, just-war theory has been severely tested. As Paul Ramsey argued, "unless there is a morality applicable to the instruments of war and intrinsically limiting its conduct . . . we must simply admit that war has no limits."[1] Unless limits are observed, warfare degenerates into murder. Michael Walzer writes, "War is distinguishable from murder and massacre only when restrictions are established on the reach of battle."[2]

Since the nineteenth century, efforts to limit the reach and brutality of war have been formalized in international protocols regarding the treatment of prisoners of war, as well as in provisions for cease-fires and surrenders. "Laws of armed conflict" have become internationally recognized and have been adopted in the codes of military conduct of most nations. For example, the U.S. Air Force Service Manual declares that military conduct must adhere to the "principle of humanity" and the "principle of military necessity." The former "forbids the infliction of suffering, injury or destruction not actually necessary for the accomplishment of legitimate military purposes."[3] The latter permits only those "measures of regulated force not forbidden by international laws which bring about the prompt submission of the enemy."[4] These two principles reflect the *jus in bello* conditions of the just-war tradition that will be explored in this chapter.

---

1. Paul Ramsey, *The Just War* (New York: Charles Scribner's Sons, 1968), 152.
2. Michael Walzer, *Just and Unjust Wars* (New York: Basic Books, 1977), 42.
3. AFP 110-31, (November, 1976), 1-5 to 1-6.
4. AFP 110-31.

The principle of noncombatant immunity has become the most important condition for the just conduct of war. Whether referred to as the principle of humanity or as the criterion of noncombatant immunity, this condition has as its intent the protection of civilians in wartime. Given the close proximity of civilians to legitimate military targets, especially in urban areas, civilian deaths are inevitable. But such "collateral damage" must not be directly intended. The principle insists that civilians may not be directly attacked. Seeking to protect civilians, the principle resists the argument that when nations make war, all their citizens contribute to the war effort and are to be regarded as combatants. This just-war condition directs our attention to the most pressing concern of modern warfare: its potential to engulf whole societies and to cause wholesale and indiscriminate destruction.[5] Nuclear targeting strategies and deterrence policies have been evaluated in light of the prohibition against intentionally attacking civilians and civilian facilities.[6] Just-war analysts not only insist on civilian immunity but specify who counts as noncombatants. Besides the obvious categories of children, the elderly, and the infirm, they include all adults not directly producing war goods (thus ruling out attacks on industries producing goods and services needed by human beings as such).[7]

In the pages that follow we will consider the manner in which the Gulf War was waged by examining the four phases of the war from the point of view of the principles of humanity and military necessity.

---

5. See, for example, James Johnson, in *Can Modern War Be Moral?* He argues that the moral onus of modern weapons is on those who must regulate their use rather than on the weapons themselves.

6. For example, see *The Challenge of Peace*, 40-57.

7. James Childress makes this distinction between goods for human use versus goods for military use in "Just-War Theories," 440.

1. The War against Iraq and Iraqi Civilians

On the evening of January 16, 1991, Americans learned of the dramatic commencement of the Gulf War. Statements from the Pentagon announced the initiation of Operation Desert Storm, and, from Riyadh, Saudi Arabia, came descriptions of the first sorties launched against Iraq at approximately 3 A.M. Baghdad time, January 17. U.S. television viewers saw what looked like a huge fireworks display illuminating the Baghdad night. In fact, the viewers were witnessing the most intensive air assault ever planned. According to its chief planner, its purpose was "to impose strategic and operational paralysis on Iraq" by attacks on "40 to 50 key strategic modes" in the opening minutes of the war in order to take away the "tools of the enemy high command."[8] Within the first 14 hours, one thousand bombing sorties and 100 cruise missiles (launched from the Persian Gulf) attacked 75 targets in and around Baghdad and Basra. In the first seven days the number of total combat missions against Iraqi targets grew to approximately 8,000. At the end of fourteen days, the total reached a staggering 15,000 bombing sorties with another 15,000 support sorties.

On January 30, 1991 General Norman Schwartzkopf declared that the Coalition had achieved "air supremacy" over Iraq.[9] "Phase One," as this period was referred to, had achieved its primary objective: disrupting Iraqi leadership control and command function while also destroying Iraq's air-defense weapon production and storage centers. Schwartzkopf offered the following specifics:

- 75 military command and control ministries and transmitting facilities, mostly in Baghdad, struck, with one-third destroyed or inoperative;

8.   Air Force Co. John Warden, interviewed in "The War We Left Behind," a documentary by Leslie and Andrew Cockburn, October, 1991.

9.   CENTCOM Briefing with Brig. Gen. Buster Glosson, Riyadh, Saudi Arabia, January 30, 1991.

- 800 sorties attacked 29 targets within the air defense system, forcing Iraq to abandon centralized control of its air defenses;

- numerous military production facilities, in and around Baghdad and Basra, destroyed;

- 1,300 sorties attacked 66 airfields, 594 aircraft shelters, and 30 fixed Scud missile facilities (plus some mobile Scud launchers);

- 500 sorties attacked 3 nuclear facilities, 18 chemical, and 10 biological weapons production facilities, and destroyed all missile production facilities.

The devastating results had rendered Iraq virtually powerless to respond. During the air attacks not a single Coalition assault aircraft had been shot down by Iraqi defense missiles.

This blitz marked the beginning of a short and intense war that some hailed as the beginning of "a new era" in the conduct of war.[10] It utilized a new generation of weapons that had the potential of sparing civilians. It was managed by military men who did not want the disproportionately high human costs of "another Vietnam."

An accurate count of the number of civilian casualties incurred in the air war may never be known. One study estimated that the number of civilians killed between January 16 and February 28 was between five and fifteen thousand, with an additional four to six thousand deaths resulting from injuries sustained during the bombings and from lack of medical care.[11] A report issued by Middle East Watch, a human rights monitoring agency, estimated that twenty-five hundred to three thousand civilians were killed as a direct result of the bombings.[12] The report criticized Coalition bombing during the

---

10. This was the claim of the House of Representatives Committee on Armed Services Committee Report "Defense for a New Era" (Washington, D.C.: U.S. Government Printing Office, 1992).

11. *On Impact*, William M. Arkin, Damian Durrant, Marianne Cherniu (Washington, D.C.: Greenpeace, 1991).

daytime, the use of nonprecision weapons, and the choice of targets which worsened food shortages and health conditions. Greenpeace, an environmental monitoring group, estimated that, in Baghdad alone, one to three thousand people died as a result of Coalition bombing.[13] The harm to civilians in Basra, Iraq's second largest city, was much greater because fewer precision weapons were used there and because it endured almost twice as many bombing raids.

Air Force Magazine summed up the Coalition's air campaign as "unprecedented in its intensity, precision, and lethality."[14] The intensity was clear enough: 88,500 tons of explosives were launched against Iraqi targets. General Schwartzkopf offered reassurance that consideration had been given to avoid noncombatants: "We're using the appropriate weapons against the appropriate targets. We're being very, very careful in our direction of attacks to avoid damage of any kind to civilian installations."[15] Other military leaders were emphatic that so-called smart bombs were utilized to avoid civilian and residential areas in and around Baghdad. 95% of the targets attacked in Baghdad were hit by allegedly "smart" bombs and missiles. Equipped with laser-guidance systems, these weapons achieved a reported 80% "hit" rate on key leadership, communications, and defense installations. But these bombs hit not only their targets (80% of the time) but also several thousand civilians unfortunate enough to be in the vicinity of Iraqi leadership and defense targets. U.S. military command described civilian deaths in Phase One as "collateral damage," the unintentional and regrettable damage to civilians accompanying the intended destruction of strategic Iraqi targets.

---

12. Middle East Watch, "Needless Deaths in the Gulf War" (Washington, D.C.: Human Rights Watch, November 17, 1991).

13. *On Impact*, 46.

14. James Canan, "Airpower Opens the Fight" *Air Force Magazine* (March, 1991), 16.

15. Gen. Norman Schwartzkopf, CENTCOM Briefing, Riyadh, Saudi Arabia, January 27, 1991.

Whatever efforts were made to spare noncombatants, the duration and ferocity of Phase One was morally troubling. In the first place, the air-war was not limited to military targets such as already described but included many key components of Iraq's civilian infrastructure. Second, despite the Coalition's declaration on January 30 of "air supremacy," attacks on the infrastructure continued until the end of the war. In addition to military targets, the air-war against Iraq targeted electric power production facilities, telephone and telecommunication centers, oil refineries and distribution centers, water purification plants (and chemical plants producing such public health necessities as chlorine), and sewage treatment facilities. Also attacked were 26 "internal state control mechanisms," the non-defense ministries of the Iraqi government. In his January 30 briefing, Gen. Schwartzkopf said that 60% of these "leadership targets" were damaged or destroyed. Although not classified as "leadership targets," also destroyed or severely damaged were Iraqi means of water purification, electrical production, fuel distribution, communication, sewage treatment and transportation facilities, including 54 rail and roadway bridges. U.S. military leaders referred to these sites as "secondary targets," explaining that they were destroyed when bombing sorties on "primary targets" had to be diverted (usually because of poor visibility).

By January 30, 33 of 36 major bridges had been bombed in almost 800 sorties. Responding to questions about attacks on electric generating plants, Schwartzkopf claimed that Coalition forces "never had any intention of destroying 100% of all electrical power. . . . Because of our interest in making sure that Iraqi citizens did not suffer unduly, we felt that we had to leave some of the electrical power in effect, and we've done that."[16] Yet, Air Force Col. John Warden later stated that the attacks were intended to knock out the power and render it irreparable in hopes of creating popular dissatisfaction against Saddam Hussein. The bombings were intensive and devastat-

---

16. Schwartzkopf, CENTCOM Briefing, Riyadh, Saudi Arabia (January 30, 1991).

ing. Workers at the Basra power plant claimed that the plant was knocked out on the second day of the war and that the first bombs struck the plant's air raid shelter, killing all seven workers inside. Although the plant was damaged beyond repair on the first raid, it was bombed twelve more times. Elsewhere in Basra, civilians testified that Coalition fighter pilots repeatedly attempted to destroy bridges in civilian quarters, in one neighborhood destroying 48 houses and killing 18 civilians.[17]

After the war, a United Nations team visiting Iraq described the damage to the country's infrastructure as "near apocalyptic" and the condition of its society as "pre-industrial." While there were some indications of the return to normalcy in Baghdad two months after the war, essential services were still lacking. Iraq was in a public health crisis six months after the war ended. A U.S. journalist reported the following conditions:

- raw sewage was still being diverted directly into Iraq's two main rivers, with no sewage treatment yet restored;

- an estimated 60% of people in southern Iraq had only contaminated water available to them;

- 2,000 cases of Typhoid per day were being reported and infectious hepatitis was at epidemic levels;

- child mortality rates in Iraq had tripled since the war.[18]

It was predicted that Iraqis would suffer the effects of the damaged infrastructure for years to come.

The destruction caused by the air war was also the result of its duration. It continued until the cease-fire on February 28, even though the Coalition had declared "air supremacy" on January 30. At a briefing on February 11, Brig. Gen. Richard Neal reiterated the U.S. policy of staying away from "civilian structures" but warned that if Iraqi military personnel moved

---

17. "The War We Left Behind."
18. "The War We Left Behind."

into civilian facilities, "they assume by international law the responsibility for the protection of any civilians that are in those structures." Neal also referred to Iraq as a "target-rich environment" — in the course of reassuring reporters that civilian areas were not being targeted.[19]

On February 12, bombing of Baghdad resumed with the intensity of the first two days of the air war. The next day Public Bomb Shelter #25 in Amiriya, on the outskirts of Baghdad, was directly hit, killing nearly all of the approximately 400 civilians inside. The explanation first offered by U.S. officials was that the shelter was being used as a government communications center. But a day later, General Thomas Kelly called the attack a mistake and offered assurances that greater care would be taken to avoid civilian structures. A likely explanation of why the shelter was hit in the first place is suggested by intelligence reports linking it to Iraqi leadership. But no Iraqi leaders were known to have been in the Shelter when it was destroyed. During the ground war, February 24-28, Baghdad had come under the heaviest attack since January 16-17 even though by then it offered fewer military targets. In its efforts to kill Saddam Hussein during the final two weeks of the war, the Coalition appeared less scrupulous about sparing civilians.

A two-fold justification was offered for the strategy of massive bombardment of military, industrial, and "public service" targets. First, such a strategy would (and did) quickly incapacitate Iraqi military capability. Second, neutralizing Iraq's potential to wage war (that is, preventing an offensive campaign against Coalition forces) prevented high casualties among Coalition forces. After the war, an Air Force "White Paper" described the Iraqi facilities that had been targeted as "vital to any nation's ability to use military power."[20] But the air-war hit facilities vital to *human life*, as well. According to a U.S. Census Bureau analyst, at least 70,000 Iraqi civilians (and

---

19. CENTCOM Briefing, Brig. Gen Richard Neal, February 11, 1991.
20. "White Paper: Air Force Performance in Desert Storm," April 1, 1991, 1-2.

as many as 90,000, according to private intelligence analysts) died as a direct result of inadequate health care and malnutrition created by the air war.[21]

So-called "surgical strikes" and "precision bombings" that are claimed to be a more humane way of waging war may actually result in higher death tolls among civilians when intense bombing occurs in urban areas. Air strikes in populated areas of Iraq resulted in extensive collateral damage. In addition, as a result of direct attacks on Iraq's infrastructure, the noncombatant death toll soared. The Coalition's objective of removing Iraqi forces from Kuwait did not justify the massive air assaults on Iraq's cities and the resulting widespread destruction of vital civilian services and economic infrastructure. To claim that water and sewage treatment facilities, telephone exchanges, electrical power plants, and food storage facilities are of "strategic military value" fails to acknowledge that they are, first of all, necessities for civilian life. In fact, after the bombings, military operations in Iraq proved to be more sustainable than civilian life because military facilities and communication systems had been "hardened." *On Impact*, the Greenpeace environmental study after the war, drew the following conclusion about the strategic bombing campaign:

> Given the availability of precision guided weapons, and the strength of the international embargo, the validity and necessity of "strategic bombing" — striking a large scale generic set of military, "economic," and national targets "rear" of the battlefield — is called into question. The embargo achieved more "strategic" purposes than the bombing, as it denied resources, spare parts, and replenishment. Iraq was not defeated because its war-making industrial base or electric power production was put out of service.[22]

---

21. The Census Bureau estimate resulted in the Bureau's attempt to fire demographer Beth Daponte. See *The New York Times*, January 9 and March 8, 1992.

22. *On Impact*, p. 147.

The study asks if the intent of the extensive bombing campaign was to demoralize the Iraqi people and undermine support for Hussein. If so, its consequences cannot be said to be "collateral," since in large part they were *intended*. They were intended to create political instability by causing widespread civilian suffering. Declaring that harm to civilians is "collateral" does not justify the deaths of or harm to civilians. Saying that a consequence was beyond one's intention may not excuse one's action. There must be evidence of positive efforts to avoid civilian damage. The proximity of civilians to possible or actual targets must be an important consideration in determining the seriousness of efforts to avoid civilian casualties. George Lopez suggests that for "collateral damage" to be morally acceptable it must be both unintended and minimal. He argues that the collateral damage inflicted on Iraqi civilians was not acceptable because it resulted from striking a list of nonmilitary targets upon which the civilian population depended for sustaining its life.[23]

Despite assurances that precautions were being taken to spare civilians, military planners of the Gulf War violated the principle of noncombatant immunity. Even those who hailed the use of "point" rather than area bombing in crowded urban areas objected to the extensive attacks on Iraq's infrastructure. Considering the damage done by the air war, Catholic ethicist John Langan wished that the civilian population could have been put "less at risk than it now seems to be" and urged that "in the future more care should be taken to protect civilians from the consequences of a catastrophic demolition of the infrastructure."[24]

If the war against Iraq is heralded as a new era in conventional warfare, the future is not bright for civilians caught in "hyper" wars — even with refinements in weapon guidance systems. Even an air war waged only with "smart bombs"

---

23. George Lopez, "Quotable Quotes, Slippery Slopes, and the Search for the Ethics of War," (published paper, 1991), 5, 25.

24. Langan, p. 365.

would not have protected a civilian society whose infrastructure was extensively targeted and intensively bombed. The bombs dropped in civilian environs of Iraq were a mixture of "smart" and "dumb" — with many more (13:1) of the latter. The precision bombing of Baghdad was, in fact, atypical, with the Pentagon itself readily admitting that only 7% of the 88,500 tons of bombs delivered in the war were precision-guided. Basra, for example, a "military town," suffered broader, less discriminating death and damage.

Some argue that in the future it may be immoral for a nation with precision bombing capability to use any other kind of weaponry in urban areas. However, the matter does not end there. Precision weaponry may offer far less of a moral breakthrough than some have suggested. Critical concerns remain. In fact, how precise are they? Regardless of how close they may come to their targets, they cannot shield civilians within their radii of destruction. In fact, the capability of precision bombing induced Gulf War targeters to "seek out the fabric of modern society: local telephone exchanges, non-military oil refineries, electrical generator plants, and civil ministries, . . . [targets] that did not stand up to the test of military necessity."[25] Urban areas and their civilian populations were not off-limits. Instead, "precision bombing" provided an air of moral legitimacy to attacks upon them.

One must conclude that there was, in fact, far too little concern for Iraqi civilians in the Gulf War. (Note that the Coalition never bombed Kuwait City to dislodge Iraqi occupiers from their strongholds.) The air campaign of "unprecedented intensity, precision, and lethality" against Iraqi society canceled to some degree the precautions taken by military commanders to spare the lives of noncombatants. Instead of immediate death, the civilian population was subjected to prolonged suffering and, in many cases, a slower death. Bryan Hehir, Professor of Christian Ethics at Georgetown University and advisor to the U.S. Catholic Conference, concluded that

---

25. *On Impact*, p. 8.

> . . . presuming both good faith and vigorous efforts to
> protect the principle of discrimination, the amount of
> destruction — combatant, civilian, material — caused
> by the air war was still appalling. The results of the
> Gulf War in this sense leave large questions unan-
> swered about the relationship between discrimination
> and proportionality, as well as how adequately the pro-
> portionality issues have been framed and pursued.[26]

During the war, Gen. Norman Schwartzkopf confessed to won-
dering whether world opinion would stop the bombing. As he
put it, "How long would the world stand by and watch the
U.S. pound the living hell out of Iraq without saying, 'Wait a
minute — enough is enough.'"[27] But the question for his own
military establishment was more to the point: What had become of the principle of humanity?

Section 2. Desert Storm and the Criterion of Proportionality

The issue of proportionality is invoked twice in just-war
theory. In the previous chapter we saw it used to determine
whether the amount of good to be achieved can be expected to
outweigh the evil war produces (this consideration was called
"strategic proportionality"). The conduct of war also requires a
calculus of how much force is necessary to achieve a military
objective. Referring to the principle of military necessity, Adam
Roberts and Robert Guelff assert "that the right of belligerents
to adopt means of injuring the enemy is not unlimited."[28]

Phases Two and Three of Operation Desert Storm began
near the end of January. Phase Two was intended to eliminate
Iraqi surface-to-air defenses in the Kuwaiti theater of operation
and was accomplished in a matter of days. Phase Three was

---

26. J. Bryan Hehir, "Just War Theory in the Post-Cold War World," presented
at the *Journal of Religious Ethics* Forum, January 12, 1992, p. 10.

27. *Newsweek*, "A Soldier of Conscience," (March 11, 1991), p. 19.

28. Adam Roberts and Richard Guelff, *Documents on the Laws of War*, Second
Edition (Oxford: Clarendon Press, 1989), 5-6.

directed at Iraqi ground forces, particularly the Republican Guard battalions, in Kuwait and southern Iraq. On the third day of Operation Desert Storm, the 150,000-strong Republican Guard was subjected to "devastating bombing by B-52s."[29] On January 30, Schwartzkopf reported that the Republican Guard in the Kuwaiti theater was the target of three hundred sorties *daily*. Fighter bombers and attack aircraft hit tanks, convoys, bunkers, and Republican Guard fortifications every three hours. U.S. military spokesmen referred to this phase as the "softening" of Iraqi troops. But after three weeks of unrelenting bombardment, the Soviet Union (one of the Coalition partners!) referred to the campaign as "Operation Desert Slaughter."[30] Indeed, during Phase Three the number of casualties among Iraqi forces was very high. Reduced to roughly half its original strength, Saddam Hussein's army was also virtually isolated from its leadership in Baghdad. A U.S. official described Iraqi forces as "basically blind" after being bombed for forty-one days.[31] Indeed, they were rendered incapable of defending themselves — to say nothing of engaging in any offensive operation.

On February 22, the United States issued an ultimatum to Iraq: withdraw all forces from Kuwait by noon, February 23, or face a ground assault by Coalition forces. Washington offered an assurance with the ultimatum: "The United States and its Coalition partners reiterate that their forces will not attack retreating Iraqi forces."[32] In the early hours of February 24, Coalition ground forces crossed the Iraqi and Kuwaiti borders from Saudi Arabia and moved toward Kuwait City. These forces met only "sporadic and ineffective" resistance from Iraqi artillery fire. One *Newsweek* pool reporter described the encounter between Coalition and Iraqi forces as follows:

---

29. *The New York Times*, January 19, 1991, A1.

30. *Isvestia* (February 19, 1991).

31. Quoted in *The Washington Post*, February 27, 1991, 28.

32. White House Press Secretary Marlin Fitzwater.

> Most Iraqis just gave up — or tried to. It was a bizarre
> scene. The advance was like a giant hunt. The Iraqis
> were driven ahead of us like animals. . . . They looked
> like spectators caught on a demolition-derby circuit.[33]

The scene was typical. The ease with which Phase Four was achieved testified to how deadly Phase Three had been.

Iraqi forces began to withdraw from Kuwait City on the night of February 24, and on the night of February 25 Baghdad Radio announced that Iraq's foreign Minister had informed the Soviet ambassador of his country's "practical compliance with U.N. Security Council Resolution 660" and of Hussein's orders to Iraqi troops to make a fighting withdrawal from Kuwait and return to the positions they had occupied before August 2, 1990. On February 26, Hussein announced that the withdrawal of Iraqi troops would be completed by that night. Later that day, Iraq complained of U.S. interference in that withdrawal. Bush angrily called Hussein's speech an "outrage" and offered his interpretation of events: "He is not withdrawing. His defeated troops are retreating. He is trying to claim victory in the midst of a rout, and he is not voluntarily giving up Kuwait." Whichever way the exodus of Iraqi troops from Kuwait was characterized, as "withdrawing" or a "retreating," it was a desperate and doomed attempt of a defeated army to escape.

On February 26, U.S. Marine and Army armored divisions entered Kuwait City. As events quickly made clear, the Coalition's plan for the liberation of Kuwait City included the destruction of retreating Iraqi troops and weapons — despite the U.S. pledge that the Coalition would not attack *retreating* Iraqi forces. U.S. divisions were positioned outside of the city to prevent the retreat and escape of Iraqi troops across the sixty mile highway to Iraq. Maj. Gen. William Keys told reporters that day: "We want to stop as many of them from retreating as possible. . . . We want to stop the withdrawal."[34] On the high-

---

33. "Move Forward and Shoot the Things," *Newsweek*, March 11, 1991, 25.

34. Maj. Gen. William Keys, 2nd Marine Division Commander, quoted by Colin Pickarson, pool reporter for *The Boston Globe*.

way between Kuwait City and Iraq — the only escape route, a death-trap was set for the retreating Iraqi troops. The method used to annihilate the 25,000 retreating Iraqi soldiers on the "Highway of Death" was described after the war:

> When Marine Corps aircraft flying close air support for ground troops arrived on the scene there was a five-vehicle wide stream of Iraqi vehicles moving on the highway out of Kuwait City. The Marines let the mass of vehicles get out of the city before attacking, and [then] laid down an aerial barrage of anti-armor mines across the road to halt the convoy. Kill zones were then assigned to groups of eight aircraft sent into the target area every fifteen minutes.[35]

According to Maj. Gen. Royal N. Moore, commander of Marine Air Wing 3, "It was a turkey shoot for several hours, then the weather turned sour." [36] *Navy Times* reported that naval aircraft flew 660 combat missions on February 27, participating in the Coalition chase of Iraqis into the trap set by ground forces. In fact, the U.S. made good the threat "to destroy every piece of equipment that [Hussein] has if we can get our hands on it."[37] U.S. reporters photographed and described in grizzly detail the miles of carnage that remained after the traffic jam had become a "turkey shoot." (After the war a representative of a major U.S. newspaper explained why very little of what reporters saw was shown back home: it would have been unpopular and even have appeared unpatriotic for the press to have shown such grotesque images. The American people did not want to think our side ever did such things.[38]) Later that day General Colin Powell recommended a cease-fire, acknowledging that if the air attacks were to continue much longer

---

35. *On Impact*, 107.

36. Mag. Gen. Royal N. Moore, in "Marines Attribute Success to Conventional Bombing," *Aviation Week and Space Technology*, 22 April 1991, 92.

37. Vice Adm. Stanley Arthur, naval commander in the Gulf, quoted by pool reporter Roman Scarborough aboard the USS Blueridge, February 27.

38. The point was made by Gene Foreman, executive director of the *Philadelphia Inquirer* in a panel discussion of press restraints during the Gulf War.

"there won't really be an enemy there."[39] A temporary cease-fire was announced to take effect at 8:00 A.M. on February 28.

As Coalition forces approached Kuwait City, Iraqi troops in and around the city had two choices: either they could disobey orders to retreat and instead surrender or they could attempt to drive the 60 miles back to Iraq. About 60,000 surrendered. But thousands attempted to retreat as they had been ordered. Reporters testified that many retreating Iraqi soldiers attempted to break from the convoys being fiercely attacked and drive back to the city and surrender. Unable to retreat or surrender, they were doomed.

Did "military necessity" dictate killing — often by burning alive — these Iraqi soldiers, estimated to number as many as 25,000? What military threat—if any—did they pose? General Merrill McPeak, Air Force Chief of Staff, explained the massacre in terms of the nature of war itself, saying:

> When enemy armies are defeated, they retreat, often in disorder, and we have what is known in the business as the exploitation phase. It's during this phase that the true fruits of victory are achieved from combat. . . . It's a tough business. . . . It often causes us to do very brutal things — that's the nature of war.[40]

The justifiable "fruits of victory" would have been the destruction of Hussein's military hardware and with it the possibility of a reconstituted Iraqi military threat to the region. Yet, on the final day of a war whose victory was assured almost from its opening hours, the Coalition had no strategy for sparing the lives of the many thousands of Iraqi soldiers whose escape route had been successfully blocked. Why had Coalition forces made no plans for the surrender of the defeated Iraqi army, something which would have involved little or no risk to its own troops? Indeed, in 1973 the U.S. government and the U.N. had successfully pleaded with the victorious Israeli army not

39. "After the Storm," *Newsweek*, March 11, 1991, p. 16.

40. Quoted in "And the Dirty Little Weapons," Paul F. Walker and Eric Stambler, *The Bulletin of the Atomic Scientists*, Vol 47, 4 (May, 1991), 22.

to engage in a "turkey shoot" against the Egyptian Third Army which Israel had encircled in the final phase of its war with Egypt.

During the final day of the Gulf War, the chain of events seemed to be determined strictly on the basis of available firepower and with little concern for the lives of Iraqi soldiers. For example, on the morning after the cease-fire, the Army's 24th Division received rocket fire (but suffered no casualties) when it encountered a large Iraqi convoy of an estimated one thousand vehicles near the Euphrates River in eastern Iraq. The convoy, with an estimated 3,000 Iraqi soldiers, was summarily destroyed. General Barry McCaffrey speculated that these Iraqi soldiers "may have been unaware of the cease-fire because U.S. forces had destroyed their lines of communication."[41] *On Impact* concluded:

> It was clear that many Iraqi units were unaware of Baghdad's order to withdraw, and later found themselves equally ignorant of the existence of a cease-fire. Iraqi soldiers who surrendered said that they had been out of communication with their commanders since the early days of the air war.[42]

Moralist John Langan articulated the moral unacceptability of massacring a defeated Iraqi army, concluding that

> It should not be impossible to work out a surrender procedure for cases like this, especially when the side receiving the surrender enjoys overwhelming superiority. Conducting a "turkey shoot" of human beings who cannot effectively defend themselves cannot be morally acceptable.[43]

Iraqi casualties, whose very large numbers the U.S. government has determined never to know, raise the question of

---

41. Quoted by Thomas Ferrard, UPI, Pool Report with the Army's 24th Division, Eastern Iraq, March 2, 1991.

42. *On Impact*, 112. The study refers to the report filed by Pool Reporter S. Lynn Wacker, *San Diego Union*, February 28, 1991.

43. John Langan, "Just-War Theory After the Gulf War," *Theological Studies*, Vol. 53, No. 1 (March, 1992), 108.

whether the U.S. military violated the fundamental principles of its own moral codes. General McPeak's explanation that doing "very brutal things" is "the nature of war," suggests a betrayal of the principle of military necessity, a principle which insists on the use of regulated force not in violation of international law and which is aimed only at reducing the risks posed by enemy forces and bringing about the enemy's "prompt submission." Among the weapons that contributed to an estimated 75,000 Iraqi casualties in the deserts of Kuwait and Southern Iraq during Phase Three were fuel air explosives (FAE's), a weapon comparable to relatively small nuclear blasts that kill in a similar fashion — by incineration or suffocation. FAEs are among a list of weapons the United Nations has proposed banning as excessively cruel and inhumane.[44]

The American people had braced themselves for a ground war that Hussein had defiantly claimed would be "the mother of all battles." But, by mid-February 1991, was it possible that U.S. military intelligence did not yet know the true capability of the Iraqi army? After the ground war began, the sheer speed of advancing U.S. tanks, plowing under Iraqi troops in their bunkers, made the surrender of the Iraqis difficult. In addition, the lack of communication between sides and within Hussein's army and the absence of any provision for the surrender of Iraqi forces contributed to the high Iraqi death toll — more than twice the number of U.S. casualties during the eight years of the Vietnam War. Although the Pentagon reported statistics of destroyed Iraqi equipment, the official policy of the U.S. government during and after the war has been to make no estimates of Iraqi casualties.

---

44. General Thomas Kelly claimed that FAEs were used primarily to detonate land mines, but others insisted that they were also used against Iraqi troops seeking shelter in desert bunkers. For a discussion of FAEs and other highly destructive anti-personnel weapons the U.S. used in the Gulf War, see Paul Walker and Eric Stambler, "And the Dirty Little Weapons," 22.

Conclusion: Will Old Principles Restrain New Wars?

The enormously destructive power of modern warfare places a heavy burden on military establishments to prosecute war with restraint and within limits. Given present war technologies, the very real danger is that war will escalate into "total war" against an entire society rather than against only its fighting forces. The overwhelming superiority that U.S. military forces exhibited over Iraq suggests still another temptation: if victory can be won so decisively and with so little risk, nations will be tempted to resort to war sooner and more often. Alan Dowty speculates:

> Sensing the possibility of a quick and satisfying military solution, planners would be tempted to use this option rather than waiting a year or more for the sanctions to play out. Furthermore, an easy military victory would lower the threshold to armed intervention in other, more dubious, cases.[45]

With the memory of the Vietnam war casting a shadow across the Middle East, a quick and decisive U.S. victory with minimal U.S. losses was seen as a political imperative. At war's end, it appeared that the mistakes of Vietnam had not been repeated. As one observer approvingly noted, in the Gulf there were no body counts, no gradualism, no micromanagement, no press interference, and no time for public protest. Indeed, the Gulf War was hailed as a new kind of war, largely because of new precision weapons which made their debut against Baghdad. But the video images were deceptive and selective: the weapons did not spare human beings and restraint was minimal, especially when Coalition victory was all but certain.

The principle of noncombatant immunity was undermined in the Gulf War. Consider again the effects of the air-war on Iraqi civilians. First, Coalition commanders offered assurances that the policy was to avoid harming civilians. However, many targets of military value located in heavily

---

45. Alan Dowty, p.29.

populated areas were attacked. The use of precision weapons to destroy targets in Baghdad undoubtedly spared the lives of many civilians. But precision weapons did not perform perfectly. Nor were they consistently used in urban areas. (93% of the weapons used against Iraq were *not* of the precision variety.) Second, the Coalition continued to wage the air war long after it had achieved air supremacy, with the apparent objective of destroying more of the infrastructure of Iraq. But since the infrastructure is essential for sustaining civilian lives, attacking it is tantamount to attacking them. Third, when the Coalition went after the Iraqi leadership, additional civilians were killed. The U.S. blamed Iraq for these deaths, arguing that Iraqi leaders had put civilians at risk by locating leadership and air defense installations near them. But the question remains: were not both sides in effect holding hostages, first Kuwaitis and then Iraqis?

The euphemism "collateral damage" is contemporary jargon for unintended civilian deaths. Such deaths entail regret but not guilt. But not every act which causes unintended civilian deaths is morally permissible. The Coalition's sustained attack on Iraq's infrastructure made the claim of "collateral damage" morally suspect. The bombing of Baghdad, Basra, and other cities was not like the carpet bombing of German cities in WW II that leveled whole cities and killed thousands of civilians. But the attacks on the urban infrastructure of Iraq were intended, and the ensuing suffering and death of Iraqis was predictable.

The principle of tactical proportionality was obscured in Operation Desert Storm — buried in the sands, if you will — as Coalition forces bulldozed through Iraqi lines. "Military necessity" allows for acts of war that subdue the enemy at minimal risk to one's own forces. But Iraqi forces were not just defeated: they were slaughtered. The fortunate Iraqi soldiers were allowed to surrender before advancing Coalition forces could kill them; thousands of others were blown to bits, buried alive, or burned to death. "Military necessity" does not permit acts of war that unduly harm enemy forces when other means of subduing them are available that do not increase the risk to one's own forces.

From its first day, the ground war was a rout. Yet the Coalition had no established plan for the surrender of Iraqi forces or for the timing of a cease-fire. An earlier cease-fire could have spared the lives of thousands of Iraqi soldiers who posed no immediate threat to Coalition forces.

The objectives for which a war is waged provide one way of determining whether its outcome will be a success. But the conduct of war contributes to those objectives and also bears upon the success or failure of a military campaign. What were the various outcomes of the Gulf War, outcomes which we might call *"post bellum"* considerations? The war freed Kuwait and vastly reduced the power of Hussein's army to menace Iraq's neighbors. It did not topple Hussein but actually contributed to a resumption of his atrocities against the Kurds and Shi'ites. George Lopez writes that, in the future, greater concern needs to be given to the "principle of timely cease-fire," which would require that a fighting power provide a "reasonable likelihood that a society can return to a minimum level of ability to meet the basic needs of its people after the conclusion of a war."[46] During the U.S. Civil War, Francis Liber authored a code of military conduct in which he wrote that military necessity "does not include any act of hostility which makes the return of peace unnecessarily difficult."[47] While this is a difficult determination to make, Lieber nonetheless recognized the danger of engendering hatred and the desire for vengeance among the vanquished. At the time of this writing, three years after the war, it is not clear that the Gulf War changed Iraq's behavior or that it had contributed to the establishment of peace in the Middle East.

---

46. George Lopez, 18.

47. Quoted by James Childress, "Francis Lieber's Interpretation of the Laws of War: General Orders No. 100 in the Context of His life and Thought," *American Journal of Jurisprudence*, 21 (1976), 49.

Questions for Reflection

1. Weapons that are heralded as "more humane" often have the opposite consequence. Why do you think that is particularly true with so-called "precision bombing" capability?

2. What political purpose was the air war against Iraqi cities intended to accomplish? Do you think that purpose was morally legitimate?

3. What is a "turkey shoot" and what moral principle does it violate? What provisions do you think should be established to protect defeated armies?

4. Do you think that developments in military technology make it impossible to observe the conditions of restraint that just-war teaching imposes?

CHAPTER FIVE

Does Just-War Theory Effectively Limit Conflict?

Introduction

In one respect, proponents of the just-war tradition might have been heartened that its conditions were discussed prior to and during the Gulf War. But not so reassuring was the fact that the tradition was invoked by various groups to provide theoretical justification both for using military force and for not resorting to it.

We have noted that the U.S. Catholic Bishops invoked just-war categories in their efforts to help form the consciences of Catholics and to influence policy makers. As a result of their analysis, many bishops in leadership positions in the U.S. Conference of Catholic Bishops urged congressional committees and President Bush to search for nonmilitary solutions to the Gulf crisis. Many bishops issued statements to their dioceses which appealed to the just-war conditions. Indeed, 28 bishops signed a statement prepared by Pax Christi, an international Catholic peace organization, which urged restraint in the Gulf.

It is difficult to judge what impact any of this had. No doubt the Bush Administration felt sufficient pressure from opponents of the war — including that voiced by Catholic and Protestant Church officials — to seek last-minute congressional approval for Operation Desert Storm. However, while the bishops had hoped to influence the politicians, they also had hoped to influence Catholic opinion. While it is also difficult to judge how successful they were in instructing the faithful on the morality of war, there is reason to doubt that their efforts changed the views of many Catholics. As the bishops themselves were aware, their opposition to the war was far from unanimous: bishops in major diocese — Cardinal Bernard Law of Boston, Archbishop James Hickey of Washington and Archbishop Joseph Ryan of the U.S. Catholic military chaplains — concluded that Operation Desert Storm was justified.[1] Archbishop Roach acknowledged and lamented the absence of a "sufficiently clear consensus [among the bishops] to offer a decisive and united judgment on the overall moral justification of this war."[2]

The bishops' difficulty in forging a "decisive and united judgment" suggests an inherent limitation of the just-war tradition, a limitation which renders it only minimally useful as a means of the moral formation of the faithful. Even its most able advocates note that the just-war conditions are difficult to apply to actual situations. According to John Langan, the *jus ad bellum* criteria provide only a "grid of formal moral concerns," and the *jus in bello* function best in retrospective evaluations of the conduct of war. While it is to be expected that moral principles are difficult to apply in concrete situations and that they may yield conflicting moral judgments, if the just-war criteria only amount to a number of formal moral claims, we might question their usefulness. When they routinely result in very different judgments, they are bound to be regarded with cynicism.

Fr. Francis Meehan observed that during the Gulf crisis few pastors offered their congregations moral guidance based on just-war considerations. According to Meehan, this happened for three reasons. First, the criteria are not suitable for

---

1. See *Origins* Vol. 20, Nos. 35, 38 (February 7 and 28, 1991).

2. Archbishop John Roach, "The War's Pastoral Challenges and Moral Questions," (February 25, 1991) *Origins* 21, 664.

sermons, presumably because they are not rooted in the Scriptures. Second, a criterion such as proportionality is very difficult to assess before the fact. Third, because just-war analysis involves political judgments, pastors are likely to be accused of being political and of injecting or imposing their own political views.[3]

As one surveys the ways in which the just-war criteria have been understood and applied, one wishes that they had more "teeth" — that is, more restrictive force. Those who see a future for the just-war theory ought to have learned something about its future potential by how it functioned in the Gulf conflict. What the Gulf episode revealed was the need to clarify and reform several of the criteria in order to make them more emphatic. I offer the following suggestions.

1. To argue "just cause" successfully requires more than demonstrating that another nation is guilty of serious injustice. It requires making a case for military intervention by *articulating just objectives and concrete means of achieving them.* Objectives must be defensive and limited to restoring the situation to the status quo prior to the crisis. Objectives must be concrete in order to be able to make antecedent determinations of proportionality. Vague objectives such as "securing a new world order" may contribute to unjustifiable escalation of military operations.

2. The criterion of legitimate authority is best served by *placing greater negotiating and policing authority with the U.N.* While the U.S. acted on the basis of U.N. Security Council Resolutions, Operations Desert Shield and Desert Storm were, in effect, U.S. operations. Thus, the first opportunity since the end of the Cold War for a U.N. response to aggression was not realized.

3. *The use of economic sanctions prior to war warrants more study.* Indeed, such sanctions may become an efficacious means of

---

3. Francis X. Meehan, "Nonviolence Today: A Pastoral Intuition Regarding its Role in the Church Today," Unpublished paper delivered at the Catholic Theological Society of America, June 1992, 5.

disabling an aggressive nation's military force. Intelligence information should be utilized to determine how effective economic sanctions will be over the course of a particular time period. The will to enforce economic sanctions against Iraq was evident in the U.N. resolutions. But the political will in the U.S. was not sufficient to sustain such sanctions.

4. The principle of noncombatant immunity can effectively protect civilians *only if restraint is present in the choice of targets and weapons,* especially in highly populated areas. Protection of civilians necessitates the implementation of international protocols in order particularly to protect infrastructures from attack.

5. Although the laws of armed conflict prohibit inflicting avoidable suffering on combatants, adequate provisions for the initiation of timely cease-fire or surrender do not exist. The way war is conducted — what is done to enemy soldiers — is a humanitarian concern requiring *international* attention. If war is part of the peace process, as theorists since Clauswitz have argued, then military operations are not antecedent to a peace process but are part of it. The way war is conducted — that is, *what is done both to civilians and to enemy soldiers* — is a major determinant of whether peace is likely to follow.

6. Finally, the just-war doctrine has more "teeth" when it leads citizens to make personal judgments regarding the morality of particular historical situations and to act on those judgments. In order for citizens to act on the basis of just-war reasoning, *nations must grant their citizens the legal right to follow their own consciences.* Citizens must be able to judge the morality of war on a case by case basis. If conscience dictates to an individual that he or she must oppose a particular war, the freedom to exercise this conscientious judgment ought to be legally recognized. At Vatican II (1963-1965) the Church urged governments to grant legal protection to conscientious

objectors. The Church also asserted that selective conscientious objection is a corollary of the just-war tradition itself. Within a year of the Council, the U.S. bishops responded to the escalating war in Vietnam by declaring that "no one is free to evade his personal responsibility by leaving it entirely to others to make moral judgments" about the moral issues raised by the war.[4] In 1968 they wrote:

> The war in Vietnam typifies the issues which present and future generations will be less willing to leave entirely to the normal political and bureaucratic processes of national decision-making.

The bishops urged citizens to scrutinize the war on the basis of the "norms . . . of the theoretical just war" and supported those whose dissent of the war was "enlightened by the message of the gospel and the teaching of the church." Such dissent, they said, was validly derived from just-war reasoning and was not merely the result of "subjective considerations."[5]

In the future one would hope to see the just-war criteria functioning with greater restrictive impact. By using the just-war tradition the Catholic Church has become an advocate for greater restraint in the use of military force to solve international disputes. The Church continues to see theoretical justification for war in situations that warrant a nation's self-defense. But it has been increasingly critical of modern warfare, from nuclear war to revolutionary violence. Convened in the shadows of the nuclear arms race and the superpowers' nuclear policy of "mutually assured destruction," the Second Vatican Council expressed "unequivocal condemnation" of "any act of war aimed indiscriminately at the destruction of entire cities or of extensive areas along with their populations."[6] At Vatican II,

---

4. National Conference of Catholic Bishops, "Statement on Peace," (Washington, D.C.: United States Catholic Conference, 1966).

5. National Conference of Catholic Bishops, "Human Life in Our Day," (Washington, D.C.: United States Catholic Conference, 1968).

6. Vatican II, *Gaudium et Spes*, Pastoral Constitution on the Church in the Modern World (1965), #80.

the bishops' sole condemnation was reserved for warfare that violates the principles of proportionality and discrimination. Pope Paul VI voiced equally strong criticism of revolutionary violence, warning that "the Church cannot accept violence and indiscriminate death as the path to liberation."[7]

The views of the present pope, John Paul II, raise the question of whether the Church is losing patience with even the theoretical possibility of justifiable war. John Paul II has expressed the strongest anti-war sentiments to be found in modern Catholic teaching. In written and spoken addresses he has called on nations to make "the most radical rejection possible of war as a means to resolve conflict."[8] Throughout the Gulf War crisis, John Paul addressed the issue of war repeatedly. While condemning Iraq's violation of "the most elementary rules of international law" and affirming the "equal rights of nations," he pleaded for means other than the use of force to restore Kuwaiti sovereignty. John Paul's consistent theme has been that war is not an effective means of obtaining justice. He argues that the use of violence produces new violence rather than justice, largely on account of the destructive power of modern warfare.

Five days before the commencement of Operation Desert Storm, John Paul told the Vatican diplomatic corps that "a peace obtained by arms could only prepare new acts of violence."[9] He continued:

> Recourse to force for a just cause would only be admissible if such recourse were proportionate to the result one wished to obtain and with due consideration for the consequences that military actions, today made more destructive by modern technology, would have for the survival of peoples and the planet itself. The 'needs of mankind' today require that we proceed resolutely toward outlawing war completely and come to

---

7. Pope Paul VI, *Evangelli Nuntiandi*, (1975), #37.

8. Pope John Paul II, Address to the Vatican diplomatic corps, 1987.

9. Pope John Paul II, Annual Address to the Vatican Diplomatic Corps, January 12, 1991, reprinted in *Origins* Vol. 20, p. 530.

cultivate peace as a supreme good to which all programs and strategies must be subordinated.[10]

John Paul then directed his appeal to Presidents Bush and Hussein personally. To Bush he wrote that "even though an unjust situation might be momentarily met, the consequences that would possibly derive from war would be devastating and tragic."[11]

John Paul appears to doubt that military means will produce more good than the evil it is designed to remedy. In short, modern war fails the test of proportionality. As John Langan acknowledges, John Paul seems to "delegitimize" resort to war.[12] Instead of military means, John Paul desires that international justice and order be achieved through dialogue and negotiation in order to address regional problems. Like his predecessors, he desires that relations between nations be conducted on the basis of international law. He also envisions a U.N. that is "increasingly and effectively furnished with coercive provisions" to enforce international laws.[13] In *Centesimus Annus*, his encyclical commemorating a century of Catholic social teaching, John Paul II expressed concern that the U.N. "has not yet succeeded in establishing, as alternatives to war, effective means for the resolution of international conflicts." He called this failure "the most urgent problem which the international community has yet to resolve."[14] Although "effective means" for resolving conflicts involve "coercive provisions," John Paul seems to rule out unilateral military undertakings.

An intriguing development for assessing the future direction of Catholic teaching on just-war is the series of editorials

---

10. Ibid, 531.

11. Pope John Paul II, Letter to President Bush, January 15, 1991, reprinted in *Origins* Vol. 20, 535.

12. John Langan, "Just War Theory After the Gulf War," *Theological Studies*, Vol. 53 no. 1 (March, 1992), 102.

13. Pope John Paul II, "Address to the Vatican Diplomatic Corps," p. 531.

14. Pope John Paul II, *Centesimus Annus*, (May, 1991), 21.

published before and after the Gulf War in *La Civiltà Cattolica*. These lengthy editorials are especially significant because the journal's close ties with the Vatican give its views semi-official status. The July 1991 editorial concluded that just-war theory is seriously flawed, that it is "untenable and needs to be abandoned."[15] The basis of its conclusion was a judgment it made about the two categories of criteria. The *jus ad bellum* conditions may theoretically be present in the form of "a war of pure defense against an aggression actually taking place." But the writers judged that observance of the *jus in bello* conditions present a practical impossibility. They note the two correctives that Spanish theologian Francisco Vittoria made to the tradition in the 16th century: first, he emphasized the requirement of proportionality; second, he recognized the danger of warfare becoming "total" in various ways (enveloping whole cultures, attacking civilian populations, and affecting several nations.) The editors of *La Civiltà Cattolica* judged that modern weaponry makes for total war and drew a strong conclusion: "We can only conclude that modern war is always immoral." To the charge that war can no longer conform to the requirements of proportionality and discrimination, they added a pragmatic consideration: war is unable to bring about greater justice but is productive of greater injustices.

These editorials draw the same practical conclusion as John Paul II. But the editors have gone a step further by suggesting that the just-war tradition is no longer viable for making moral decisions about the use of force in international conflict because of *the nature of modern warfare*. More than ever before, the just-war tradition is itself being challenged — and with it, the possibility of a "just war."

Langan is indeed correct in his assessment that the *La Civiltà Cattolica* was

> attempting a revision and repositioning of official
> Catholic teaching so that the strong denunciations of

---

15. "Christian Conscience and Modern Warfare" *La Civiltà Cattolica* (July, 1991). Quotation is from the translation by William Shannon in *Origins* 21, 450-455.

warfare issued by recent popes would count as the center of the teaching, and defensive war against ongoing aggression would count as a remote peripheral exception.[16]

Events since the Gulf War have continued to raise the issue of the usefulness of armed intervention and the urgent need for effective negotiations between nations and between warring factions within nations. Recent conflicts in Bosnia and Somalia provide sobering lessons about the limits of armed counterforce and the necessity of negotiations among conflicting parties.

The ethnic war that broke out in 1992 between Serbs, Croatians, and Muslims has claimed 200,000 lives and displaced a million people. International efforts to pressure Bosnian Serb rebels to stop their aggression have proved futile. Despite efforts of the U.N. to declare several "safe areas" to protect Bosnian Muslims, Bosnian Serbs laid siege to six cities, including Sarajevo. By late 1993, the Serbs had gained control of approximately 70% of the country. The Bosnian Serb campaign of "ethnic cleansing" was interpreted by many as outright genocide. The U.N., with the support of NATO forces, imposed an embargo on all arms bound for Bosnia. Some criticized the embargo because it prevented the Bosnian government and its Muslim majority from defending themselves. But the idea of creating "a level playing field" by arming the Bosnian Muslims seemed to many only to flame the war and bring about more deaths on all sides. Instead, the U.N. committed peacekeeping forces to attempt to maintain the flow of humanitarian assistance and to protect international relief workers. The humanitarian mission was also criticized for not providing effective protection to Bosnian civilians who were subjected to continuous attacks from Serbian artillery positions surrounding Bosnian cities. Finally, the U.N. urged a negotiated settlement that would partition Bosnia into three small ethnic republics, a solution that the Bosnian government has refused to consider. In

---

16. Langan, 103.

February 1994, a particularly bloody mortar attack on a Sarajevo marketplace led the U.N. and NATO to issue an ultimatum to the Serbs: either withdraw or commit to the U.N. all
heavy artillery from positions surrounding the city or risk air
strikes. Fearing that NATO would actually carry out its threat
this time and urged to comply by the Russians, the Serbs withdrew their artillery. The remaining question is how the Serbian, Croatian, and Muslim factions will decide that the time
has come to accept a negotiated settlement.

The civil war in Somalia has contributed to massive star-
vation and impeded the flow of humanitarian aid into the
country. In 1993, a United Nations peacekeeping force and U.S.
troops conducted a protective police action to allow humanitarian aid to reach starving Somalians. Initially, the international intervention was only for humanitarian purposes.
However, its objective was expanded to include a manhunt for
Mohammed Farrah Aidid, leader of one of the feuding clans.
In retaliation, Somali clansmen killed 18 U.S. servicemen. With
little support at home for this U.S. intervention, the Clinton administration set a six-month deadline for the removal of all
U.S. forces from Somalia.

Of particular interest was the resolution approved by the
U.N. Security Council in February 1994, which scaled down the
U.N. peacekeeping mission in Somalia. The mission was no
longer authorized to disarm Somalian factions with force but
had the limited duty of protecting relief workers and U.N. officials while also guarding airports and roads necessary for dis-
tributing relief supplies. One of the drafters of the resolution,
the U.S. Ambassador to the U.N., Madeleine Albright, declared
that "the people of Somalia must bear the responsibility for national reconciliation and reconstruction . . . and [must] pursue
all opportunities to resolve their differences peacefully."[17]

Humanitarian concern for the massive suffering of Bosnians
and Somalians makes a strong case for military intervention as a
way to stop the fighting. But the contemplation of the use of air

17. Reported in the *Milwaukee Journal*, (February 5, 1994), A18.

strikes against the Bosnian Serbs has raised a host of fears in European capitals, in Washington, and in the U.N., that such a course of action might increase the level of hostilities. The Clinton administration was quick to claim that the objective of the ultimatum was modest: it was not expected to end the war or even the siege of Sarajevo, but only to stop mortar attacks against the city. The Administration also admitted that effective air strikes against these Bosnian positions would not nullify Serbian threats elsewhere in Bosnia. The threatened air strikes were clearly not offered as a panacea; instead, the President publicly acknowledged the risks: the Serbs might become even less willing to talk and might escalate their attacks on Sarajevans and also attack international peacekeepers and relief workers. Also, Serbian artillery might prove very difficult to destroy. If so, the need for follow-up ground action would still exist.

In effect, what the Administration offered was a specific and limited objective of the sort that is necessary to pass the tests of just cause and calculations of proportionality. Just-war theory is intended to be a restraint against military intervention for whatever purposes, even altruistic and humanitarian ones. James Johnson has put the matter well, and I quote him at length:

> What makes the case of intervention by force for humanitarian purposes so hard is that such moral justification may be greatly compelling, and yet we still, in a given case, should not intervene by military force. There may not be the necessary authority to do so; there may be no reasonable hope of success; military intervention may produce more harm than good; other means of dealing with the crisis at hand may be more effective; and some forms of military intervention may hinder the cause of peace rather than serving it. . . . Requiring reasonable hope of success, along with last resort, serves as a reminder that military forces should not be seen as a cure-all for ills that other methods have not been able to remedy. The mere fact that non-military forms of humanitarian aid have been tried and failed in a given case does not mean that military forces should now be committed; in the case at hand

86 • *Peacemaking Christians*

they may not work either or may make for a worse
situation. The truth is, moreover, that armies, navies,
and air forces are not created for this as their primary
purpose. For the United States military, that purpose is
our national defense, and the services are structured
accordingly.[18]

The lack of success in ending the Bosnian and Somalian conflicts suggests that we are far from possessing effective ways of
defusing nationalistic and ethnic conflicts before the cycle of
killing spins out of control. While we threaten to take military
action against the aggressors, our intuition is that more military action will only serve to escalate and prolong the conflict.
While there is a deep sense of futility that military solutions
cannot remedy the terrible injustices being committed before
our very eyes there is also a casting about for untapped ways
of beginning to knit a fragile peace.

In February 1994, the Clinton Administration proposed
Presidential Directive 13 that reversed an earlier policy of deploying small "rapid deployment forces" to global hotspots.
PDR13 established more stringent criteria for engagement of
U.S. military forces. It specified that before action could be
taken there must be evidence of an international security risk
or of a gross violation of human rights. It also required that
U.S. forces must be part of a multinational effort but stipulated
that they accomplish their mission under U.S. command.

Conclusion

After the Gulf War, U.S. military strategists were con-
gratulated by some for not repeating the mistakes of Vietnam.
Indeed, they had fought a new kind of war with lasers, infra-
red see-in-the-dark-glasses for night bombing, fuel-air explosives, and a new generation of bombers and missiles. But the
end of the war raised many questions: Had things changed
much in Iraq or the Middle East? Hadn't western nations

---

18. James Johnson, "The Just War Idea and the Ethics of Intervention"
(Colorado Springs, Colo.: U.S. Air Force Academy, 1993), 15, 17-18.

helped Hussein build the most deadly arsenal in the Middle East in the first place (although that revelation appears to have had little effect on continuing arms sales)? While the Gulf War appeared to be a triumph of new war technologies, it did not contribute to greater justice or a more stable peace in the Middle East. Even the disarming of Saddam Hussein proved to be short-lived. The central moral question after the war is whether long-held moral convictions embedded in just-war conditions are adequate for restraining future conflicts. Whether just-war criteria will be reformed is a question of how seriously we are willing to take the tradition.[19] If the criteria are not more stringently applied, then other less ethical concerns will govern our use of military force: efficiency and expediency will come to justify the use of whatever technology we have at hand to "win" with minimal loss of life (to our side) and with minimal political fallout. In effect, the just-war tradition will be cast aside.

Whether in the case of the Persian Gulf War or the Somalian or Bosnian civil wars, what is notably missing in the U.S. is sustained public debate concerning the use of military force as a means of restoring peace. *How* to restore peace is an essential debate. As Johnson warns, we ought not put "our military forces on the line without a clear understanding of how their sacrifice will serve the cause of peace in the situation at hand."[20]

With numbing regularity wars erupt and partisans on all sides proclaim with fanatic zeal the justness of their causes. All too regularly they make hostages out of civilians in their fratricidal wars. Citizens are shot, starved, raped, and become refugees. Those who commit these crimes often lose their own moral moorings, becoming spiritual casualties of the war. As a Serbian sniper in the hills above Sarajevo described his own sense of self-loss and damnation:

---

19. John Howard Yoder reminds those who adhere to the tradition that its logic even commits them to accept the possibility of surrender rather than to violate its principles. See *When War is Unjust: Being Honest in Just-War Thinking* (Minneapolis, MN: Augsburg Press, 1984), Ch. 5.

20. Johnson, "The Just War Idea and The Ethics of Intervention." 19.

I have no feelings for what I do. I have no life
anymore. I go from day to day, but nothing means anything. I don't want a wife and children. I don't want
to think.[21]

We can blame the snipers, the soldiers, and the politicians
for wars. But what are we, the citizenry, doing to promote solutions to conflicts that do not entail resorting to war?

Although we have concerned ourselves with renewing the
just-war tradition, a more radical question is suggested by recent Catholic teaching that has stopped just short of repudiating all war. What alternatives for restraining violence are there
besides the just-war tradition? Have we limited our imaginations so much that we believe that we are "stuck" with war?
For some Christians, the first step toward finding other alternatives has been to repudiate war and to commit themselves to
other ways of seeking peace.

Questions for Reflection

1. What is Pope John Paul II's position on modern war? Do
you think he is saying something new?

2. Consider how people are trained to be police professionals
and to be military professionals. In what ways are they
trained quite differently? What are the difficulties of using
militart forces to perform police functions or humanitarian
funcitons?

3. How would you respond to the assertion that war is "part
and parcel of the human condition" and that we are indeed
"stuck" with it?

4. How might the Catholic Church have been more effective in
urging restraint during the Gulf crisis? How do you think it
might be more effective in restraining future warmaking?

---

21. "A Sniper's Tale," *Time* (March 14, 1994), 24.

CHAPTER SIX

Christian Pacifism (Reconsidered)

Introduction

In its official teaching the Catholic Church has increasingly opposed war. By invoking the just-war criteria, the present pope has reached what appears to be a pacifist conclusion that, under present conditions, war is no longer a morally legitimate option for Christians. Is this to be understood as a turn toward pacifism in contemporary Catholic teaching? Given the fact that Catholics have often patriotically supported their government leaders, is it likely that they will develop an abiding suspicion toward war? Pacifists are often a maligned minority whom the majority does not readily tolerate in wartime. Often pacifists are regarded as naive and idealistic or as socially irresponsible misfits. For refusing to bear arms, they are suspected of cowardice and are accused of complicity with injustice for not coming to the aid of those who suffer injustice. In short, they are regarded as "nay-sayers" who offer no effective alternatives to the use of military force. The animus that arises towards those who oppose war was again manifested during the Gulf War. For example, a Nebraska pediatrician who objected to the war while in Saudi Arabia with her reserve unit received a dishonorable discharge and later had her state medical license revoked on the grounds that she was of "unfit moral character" to practice medicine. In wartime, pacifism is viewed as tantamount to sympathizing with the enemy.

This chapter will examine pacifism both in modern Catholicism and in popular sentiment. Section One describes the opening toward pacifism seen in Catholic teaching. It also includes a brief survey of the pacifism of earlier eras of Christianity. Section Two probes the relationship between the pacifist and just-war positions. Our goal will be to clarify pacifist convictions by addressing the confusions and caricatures that surround this moral position. There are a great variety of convictions, both secular and religious, that are identified as "pacifist." While it is not possible to represent "what every pacifist believes," two features of pacifism in the Catholic tradition can be identified. First, pacifism is the belief that violence and killing in war is wrong. Pacifism repudiates war. However, those who hold this position need not necessarily renounce the use of force in other contexts (e.g., by the police, by citizens in self-defense). Second, pacifism entails the commitment to use non-violent means to defend innocent persons, resolve conflicts, reconcile opponents, and reform political systems. Beyond these two convictions, pacifism admits of considerable variety.

1. Pacifism in Contemporary Catholicism

Throughout the twentieth century Catholic social teaching has encouraged social action on behalf of international cooperation to bring about peace, justice, and the defense of rights in the face of totalitarianism.

In the late nineteenth century, Pope Leo XIII (1878-1903) personally mediated several international disputes. He also endorsed the international peace movement and various Catholic peace organizations that had arisen in Europe prior to World War I.[1] His successor, Benedict XV (1914-1922), used his personal wealth as well as that of the Vatican to assist victims

---

1. Ronald Musto, *The Catholic Peace Tradition* (Maryknoll, NY: Orbis Books, 1986), 171, 177. James Johnson observes that "unstable unions" of Christian pacifists and international utopians flourished in the late nineteenth century but declined sharply with the outbreak of World War I. See Johnson, *The Quest for Peace*, 232. In the 1920s and 1930s the pattern was repeated.

of the Great War — civilians, combatants, and prisoners of war. Pope Pius XI (1922-1939) protested the rearmament within Europe and urged a "peace of justice" rather than the "state of armed peace which is scarcely better than war itself."[2] Also, throughout the 1930s Pius XI condemned the policies of Nazism and fascism.[3]

When war broke out again in September, 1939, Pope Pius XII (1939-1958) denounced both Nazi and Soviet aggression. As we noted in the last chapter, a dominant theme in Pius's papacy was the threat that war posed to international order. His negative appraisal of war found expression in his narrowing of the criterion of just cause to permit only self-defense and defense of others under unjust attack. It was Pius who argued that those unjustly attacked ought to "suffer the injustice" rather than undertake an armed conflict that would do disproportionate harm.[4]

While modern popes were increasingly critical of war and committed to diplomatic means of resolving international conflict, pacifism still aroused suspicion. For instance, Pius XII urged vigilance and active self-defense against communist regimes. In the wake of the aborted Hungarian revolt, he wrote:

> May God arouse you from your lethargy, keep you free from all complicity with tyrants and warmongers, enlighten your consciences, and strengthen your wills in the work of reconstruction.[5]

Apparently, Pius never dreamt that 25 years later the Polish people would wage a successful nonviolent revolt against their captors.

---

2. Pius XI, *Ubi Arcano Dei.*

3. Musto, 174-175.

4. Pius XII, "War and Peace," an address to delegates to the eighth congress of the World Medical Association, September 30, 1954, in *Patterns of Peace: Catholic Statements on International Order,* ed. Harry Flannery (Westminster, MD: Newman Press, 1962), 237.

5. Quoted in Musto, 185.

At the Second Vatican Council (1963-1965) the Catholic Church for the first time in its modern history expressed admiration for those who choose a pacifist course:

> . . . we cannot fail to praise those who renounce the use of violence in the vindication of their rights and who resort to methods of defense which are otherwise available to weaker parties too . . . .

To this was added the qualification:

> . . . provided that this can be done without injury to the rights and duties of others or of the community itself.[6]

Here was a two-fold position upholding, on one hand, the right of individuals to renounce the use of force and, on the other hand, the right of nations to defend themselves with arms. The Council maintained a distinction between private and public moral roles, construing pacifism as a commendable stance for individuals but not for those charged with the defense of the community. Richard Miller describes the pacifism endorsed at the Council as a "human rights-based pacifism," because it affirmed the desirability of defending rights by non-violent means.[7] In addition to praising the pacifist commitment, the Vatican Council called for nations to grant legal status to and make "humane provisions for . . . those who, for reasons of conscience, refuse to bear arms provided, however, that they accept some other form of service to the human community."[8]

Two factors were at work to bring about the endorsement of pacifism at Vatican II: first, the witness of small numbers of Catholic pacifists and, second, the ferocious nature of modern war — especially of nuclear war. The number of Catholics who refused military service on pacifist grounds during the First and Second World Wars was very small. Gordon Zahn estimates that the number of U.S. Catholic pacifists dur-

6. *The Pastoral Constitution on the Church in the Modern World*, Par. 78.

7. Richard Miller, *Interpretations of Conflict* (Chicago: University of Chicago Press, 1991), Ch. 3.

8. Par. 79.

ing World War II was approximately 225.[9] Even many members of the Catholic Worker movement abandoned the pacifist position of founder Dorothy Day during the War.[10] In Austria, one lone Catholic, Franz Jaegerstaetter, refused to be inducted into Hitler's army. After being tried and imprisoned, he was executed for his refusal on August 9, 1943. Jaegerstaetter's local pastor and even his bishop had tried to convince him that he was acting irresponsibly by taking personal responsibility for judging Hitler's war. Although Jaegerstaetter's case did not become widely known until the 1960s, his courageous commitment to his conscience (and the witness of a handful of other Catholics in other times and places) has influenced the position of the Church.[11]

In their assessment of modern war, the Council fathers expressed fear of "weapons [which] can inflict massive and indiscriminate destruction far exceeding the bounds of legitimate defense."[12] They urged all citizens to consult their consciences, and especially to resist any immoral commands that might result in crimes of war. The Bishops grounded peace in respect for peoples' dignity, in justice, and in love, urging Christians "to practice the truth in love" (Eph. 4:15) and "to join with all true peacemakers in pleading for peace and bringing it about."

We have already noted that the Council's appeal to conscience was reemphasized by the U.S. Catholic Bishops a few years later when they urged Catholics to morally evaluate the war in Vietnam by means of the just-war categories. The bishops also urged the U.S. government to grant legal recognition of the right of people of good conscience to refuse to serve in the war if they judged that it did not meet the conditions of justifiable war. In 1976 the bishops again advocated legal recognition of those who objected to particular wars on the basis

---

9. Gordon Zahn, *Another Part of the War: The Camp Simon Story* (Amherst: University of Massachusetts Press, 1979).

10. Dorothy Day, *The Long Loneliness* (New York: Curtis Books, 1952).

11. For the most complete account of the Jaegerstaetter case, see Gordon Zahn, *In Solitary Witness* (Collegeville, MN: Liturgical Press, 1977).

12. *The Pastoral Constitution on the Church in the Modern World* (1965), 80.

of just-war analysis (a position called "selective conscientious objection").

In 1983 the U.S. Catholic Bishops endorsed pacifism with an enthusiasm unprecedented in modern Catholicism. Within months they were joined by many other Bishops' Conferences around the world. That year the U.S. Bishops wrote *The Challenge of Peace*, a pastoral letter on peace and war in the nuclear age. They declared that a "new moment" in Church teaching regarding just-war and pacifism had arrived:

> While the just-war teaching has clearly been in posses-
> sion for the past 1,500 years of Catholic thought, the
> "new moment" in which we find ourselves sees the
> just-war teaching and non-violence as distinct but inter-
> dependent methods of evaluating warfare. They di-
> verge on some specific conclusions, but they share a
> common presumption against the use of force as a
> means of settling disputes. Both find their roots in the
> Christian theological tradition; each contributes to the
> full moral vision we need in pursuit of peace. We be-
> lieve the two perspectives support and complement one
> another, each preserving the other from distortion. Fi-
> nally, in an age of technological warfare, analysis from
> the viewpoint of non-violence and analysis from the
> viewpoint of the just-war teaching often converge and
> agree in their opposition to methods of warfare which
> are in fact indistinguishable from total warfare.[13]

The Bishops described commitments to just-war and to nonviolent activism as "complementary."[14] Presumably, the

---

13. Par. 120-121.

14. Neither just-war advocates nor pacifists were altogether happy with the formulation. James Finn charged that pacifists' use of just-war doctrine "define[d] its tenets so narrowly as to strangle it." "Pacifism and Just War: Either or Neither," in *Catholics and Nuclear War*, Philip J. Murnion, ed. (New York: Crossroad, 1983), 143. He had in mind those criteria involving difficult judgments that we discussed in Chapter Three: proportionality, last resort, and reasonable hope of success. On the other hand, pacifist Gordon Zahn lamented that the bishops had not conveyed the spirituality of pacifism and that their advocacy of nonviolence might be "too little . . . and too late." Gordon Zahn, "Pacifism and the Just War," in *Catholics and Nuclear War*, 120.

two positions remind us of the demands of justice (not to be ignored by pacifists) and the presumption against life-taking (easily forgotten by those who seek to justify war). The bishops noted the sources of convergence between just-war and pacifism. First, both positions "share a common presumption against the use of force as a means of settling disputes." Second, the potential of modern warfare to escalate into "total war," in violation of the principles of discrimination and proportionality, leads to a very restrictive justification of the use of force. While the bishops acknowledged the right of nations to defend themselves, they expressed grave reservation about the morality of modern war, especially nuclear war.[15]

Thus, the position they took on nuclear policy was virtually one of nuclear pacifism insofar as they concluded that both the first use of nuclear weapons and retaliatory strikes were morally prohibited.[16]

The Challenge of Peace roundly praised pacifism's commitment to nonviolence. The bishops no longer endorsed pacifism as only a private option, but instead commended "serious and continuing study" to develop programmed methods for both individuals *and nations* "to defend against unjust aggression without using violence."[17] They praised nonviolent resistance as offering "a common ground of agreement" between just-war and pacifist positions since both "testify to the Christian conviction that peace must be pursued and rights defended within moral restraints and in the context of other basic values."[18] They noted the means available to nonviolent resisters, includ-

---

15. See *The Challenge of Peace*, par. 71, 75-77, 80, 83, 93, 120. Miller argues that the Bishops offer a version of just cause more narrow than Pius XII's. He contends that because of their fear of the ferocity of war and the potential anarchy to which it may lead, the bishops demanded that "as a condition for going to war, one must be reasonably certain, *prospectively*, that the methods of war will stand within *in bello* restrictions" (66); see *The Challenge of Peace*, par. 101.

16. *The Challenge of Peace*, para. 144, 147, 148, 151, 158, and 161.

17. Par. 77.

18. Par. 224 and 74.

ing "popular defense instituted by government . . . [using] peaceable non-compliance and non-cooperation . . . [for] blunting the aggression of an adversary [and] winning the other over."[19] The bishops declared that "work to develop non-violent means of fending off aggression and resolving conflict best reflects the call of Jesus both to love and to justice."[20]

The U.S. bishops were soon joined by other Bishops' Conferences. In May 1983, the Dutch bishops' conference asserted that "the development of methods which enable people to resist injustice and to defend themselves without using violence is in keeping with the spirit of the Gospel and may not be labelled as utopian and unrealistic." The Japanese bishops wrote: "It is self-evident that our endeavors for peace must be nonviolent." The German bishops claimed that "the Christian ethos of love must become effective also . . . in international politics" by trying "to win over the opponent of peace, discover non-violent solutions to conflicts and offer fields of cooperation."[21] The bishops of Belgium reflected: "Maybe the Church of earlier times and of today should have given more emphasis to the witness of nonviolence." At the very time official church teaching was commending pacifism, Catholics and Protestants in numerous places and political contexts throughout the world were waging nonviolent struggles for justice and peace and demonstrating the practical effectiveness of pacifism. The next chapter will explore the twentieth century emergence of nonviolent resistance as a growing form of practicable pacifism.

The human rights-oriented pacifism that has emerged in modern Catholic social teaching captures the central concerns of Catholic morality. It emphasizes the prohibition against harm and the duty to defend the innocent. Rights-based pacifism is not to be equated with nonresistance. While it advocates nonviolent means of defense, it also acknowledges the

---

19. Par. 223,225.

20. Par. 78.

21. "Out of Justice, Peace" (April, 1983)

duty of pacifists to defend the community (nonviolently). Miller argues that the advocacy of pacifism in contemporary Catholicism is the result of rethinking the relationship between justice and "peace-as-order" (the latter being Augustine's legacy). As Miller describes it (and recalling Pius XII), in the shadow of modern war, the tradition has reached the conclusion that "for the sake of peace we may be required to suffer voluntarily rather than reciprocate an act of violence."[22] Christians may be required "to suffer injustice" rather than vindicate their rights through recourse to war which does disproportionate harm to human lives and cultures and the natural environment.

Richard Miller observes that appreciation of pacifism has grown with the sober realization of the awful consequences of modern warfare. Under these conditions, Miller writes, the Church concedes that "the pacifist is allowed to judge the means [of modern warfare] to be disproportionate to the end of self-defense."[23] In our discussion of strategic and tactical proportionality, we noted that calculations must be done and that they are often not easy to do. An undeniable feature of modern armed conflicts is that in the process of defending innocent persons they have caused great disproportionate harm. The devastating effects of armed force which does not sufficiently discriminate between combatants and noncombatants has contributed to a convergence between the just-war and pacifist positions. Especially in the age of nuclear weapons and more devastating conventional weaponry, doubts have grown whether modern weaponry can be used with sufficient restraint. The carpet bombing of German cities, the nuclear bombing of Hiroshima and Nagasaki, and the cold war nuclear strategies of the 1960s and 1970s all demonstrated the movement toward engaging in "total war." These developments led the Second Vatican Council to utterly condemn the "weapons of mass destruction" and the "inexorable chain of events" that

---

22. Miller, 64.
23. Ibid., p. 82.

lead to the violations of proportionality and noncombatant immunity once war has begun. "Just-war pacifists" now use the *jus in bello* categories to conclude that the conditions of modern warfare necessarily violate the principle of proportionality.

The question of the normative status of pacifism within contemporary Christianity is often linked to the question of whether pacifism was normative for the earliest Christian witnesses and communities. Historians of Christianity have attempted to weigh the evidence for pacifism throughout various periods. Their conclusions often bear the biases of their own church affiliation. This is especially true of studies of the first four centuries undertaken by historians associated with the peace churches spawned by the radical reformation. James Johnson charges that the "standard pacifist accounts" attempt to line up evidence for a univocal embrace of pacifism in the "pure" centuries of the tradition, followed by the "corruption" of the tradition after the time of Constantine. Johnson and other scholars (with their own just-war bias) have reexamined the early centuries of Christianity. Having examined the evidence of the first century and a half, Johnson has concluded that we are able to reconstruct the social background but not the specific details of Christian views regarding war and military service.[24] He reminds us that the first Christians expected the imminent return of Jesus and the arrival of the Kingdom of God he had proclaimed. Believing that the world was soon to end, they invested themselves in the world to come. As a result, non-Christians considered the civic loyalty of Christians suspect, especially because the latter refused to worship the gods that were thought to guarantee Rome's well-being. For their alleged disloyalty, early Christian communities became targets of periodic and, at times, intense persecution until the fourth century.

---

24. James Johnson, *The Quest for Peace: Three Moral Traditions in Western Cultural History* (Princeton, N.J.: Princeton University Press, 1987), 33. See also John Helgeland, Robert J. Daly, and J. Patout Burns, *Christians and the Military: The Early Experience* (Philadelphia: Fortress Press, 1985).

No doubt there were theologians who espoused a thoroughgoing withdrawal from the defense of the Empire. For example, Tertullian (ca. 200), Clement of Alexandria (ca. 200), and Origen (ca. 248) all insisted on the essential peaceableness of Christianity. In *Against Celsus*, Origen refuted charges that Christians were disloyal to the Empire, by pointing out that they supported it and prayed for the well-being of the emperor. However, he argued that monotheism prohibited Christians from participating in Roman religion. Tertullian (ca. 200) displayed a definite hostility toward Roman life and urged his fellow Christians to separate themselves from pagan culture. But Johnson does not judge that these patron saints of pacifism were representative of the entire period. Instead, he sees Clement, Origen, and Tertullian as representing one strand "in the pluralistic fabric of developing Christian thought on war during the early centuries of the Church."[25]

The pluralism of which Johnson speaks appears in the variety and evolution of attitudes Christians had toward certain professions, especially military life, and certain trades associated with Roman religious cults (e.g., gold and silversmiths producing cultic objects). For example, the initial Christian attitudes toward the Roman army may have been one of disinterest, reflecting the geographical and social location of Christians, who were concentrated in urban areas — while military recruitment occurred primarily in rural areas. Christians belonged to social groups not likely to be recruited for service in the legions. Johnson argues that as early as the second century, Christians were found in the ranks of the Roman army and that some but not all Christians viewed military service as a problem. Furthermore, the number of Christians in the Roman army rose steadily until the end of the second century when the number of Christians in the legions was large. Johnson argues that soldiers who converted to Christianity would not have been inclined to leave military service both because of the harsh penalties for doing so and because Roman

25. Johnson, p. 29.

authorities would not have wanted to lose manpower by eliminating them.

Those Christians who did oppose the military profession could have been opposed on a number of grounds. First, the association of army life with idolatry was strong, especially with the advent of the cult of emperor worship in the third century. Second, military life had a reputation for immorality. Third, Christianity maintained a strong prohibition against life-taking and bore the memory of Jesus' refusal to take up the sword in self-defense. But the picture appears to be a mixed one: on the one hand, increasing participation by some Christians in military life; on the other hand, opposition to military service by others.

By the late fourth century the social and political situation of Christians was again changing. Those who argue that pacifism did not dominate early Christianity also take issue with the thesis that Emperor Constantine's embrace of Christianity effectively led to the compromise of Christianity as it accommodated itself to the world and began to enjoy the fruits of political power. Indeed, the empire not only made peace with Christianity but granted it privileged status. Christians came to associate their own welfare with the stability of the empire — and that stability was being challenged externally by powerful barbarians in the north and internally by social malaise. As we noted in an earlier chapter, in the early fifth century St. Augustine, Bishop of Hippo in North Africa, argued that Christians shared the duty of defending a just and well-ordered Roman society, by which an "earthly peace [would] bear upon the peace of heaven."[26] Augustine approved of the military profession, provided that its object was to preserve and restore harmonious social order and its practitioners behaved virtuously. Augustine viewed the defense of innocent persons and the preservation of public order as part of the commandment to love one's neighbor.

---

26. St. Augustine, *The City of God*, Book Nineteen.

With the break-up of the Empire and the loss of strong centralized authority, regional violence escalated. In the Middle Ages, the Church attempted to restrain war-making by practices such as the "truce of God" and "peace of God" and by banning certain weapons. In addition, the Church prescribed rigorous penances for killing or harming in battle, a reminder to soldiers of the gravity of killing (even though the larger moral responsibility belonged to the rulers rather than to their subjects who fought at their command).

In the Middle Ages, monastic movements brought a renewal of "peace movements" to the church, as Christians embraced the monastic way of life and rejected the violence of the secular world. In the tenth century, Waldensians and Cathars preached that all Christians were strictly prohibited from engaging in violence. Peace movements were also given impetus by the thought of utopian thinkers like Dante and Marsilius of Padua who envisioned a pan-European world order in which war itself would be eliminated. Johnson argues that the twelfth century marked the beginning of a coherent and continuous tradition of pacifism in Western Christianity which took two forms: (1) a utopian pacifism whose adherents envisioned a world government in which wars between nations would be avoided; and (2) a religious sectarian pacifism whose adherents rejected the violence of the political order and withdrew from it. On the eve of the Reformation, the Italian humanist, Erasmus, offered such a utopian vision. During the Reformation, "radical reformers" such as the Anabaptists (Swiss Brethren) in their effort to recover the moral rigor of the early church rejected violence. This marked the institutionalization of Christian sectarian pacifism. Johnson traces these two trajectories into the modern period, focusing on radical Protestant pacifism, the "perpetual peace" movements of the Enlightenment, and the English evangelical Protestant pacifism of the eighteenth century.[27] Within Catholicism, the just-war theory solidified between the sixteenth and nineteenth centuries with the

---

27. Johnson, Chapters 4 and 5.

result that few Catholic pacifist voices were heard in the early modern period.[28]

What conclusions can we draw from this brief survey? First, contrary to what some modern Christians believe, there may never have been a "golden age" of pacifism. Indeed, the pacifism that did exist at the time was part of a world-view different from that held by contemporary Christians: the early Christians expected the world to end soon. For several generations they lived as a marginal minority within Roman society. When expectation of the immanent end of the world faded and with newly acquired status in the empire, Christian "stake" in the Roman social world made them view the invading "barbarians" as almost a cosmic threat, something to be resisted. As the church opposed the proliferation of wars and deadlier weapons in the Middle Ages, peace movements sprang up. Since the time of the Reformation, certain communities of Christians vigorously protested that it was unfitting for believers to engage in violence.

Second, we may conclude that, even though there has not been a golden age of pacifism, there have always been Christian pacifist witnesses who believe that their faith requires them to refuse to use violence. Rather than seek authority for contemporary Christian pacifism in the practices of earlier periods of Christianity, we are better off examining the basis for Christian pacifism in our own time. Thus, we have looked at the emergence of pacifism within Roman Catholicism in this century, a development especially remarkable because of the Catholic Church's long identification with the just-war tradition.

2. Beyond the Caricatures: Pacifism Reconsidered

Despite the praise of pacifism found in recent official Catholic pronouncements, pacifism is still viewed with disdain by many people. So negative is the common view of pacifism

---

28. See Musto, Ch. 11.

that even people who have opposed war and embraced non-violence have sought to avoid the label "pacifist" for their position. Gandhi, for example, protested that the word connoted an incapacity to act leading to the loss of self-respect. He spoke instead of "nonviolent resistance" to describe his disposition to attack injustices through a variety of nonviolent means. We might be well-advised to follow him in abandoning the word "pacifism" if it cannot be freed of its association with "passivity." The effective campaigns of nonviolence resistance we shall describe in the next chapter bear no resemblance to solitary protesting individuals or politically alienated and powerless minorities living on the edges of society.

Let us consider what unites and what separates pacifist and just-war convictions, rather than assume that they are absolutely irreconcilable positions. Imagine how the two positions might represent themselves:

The non-pacifist:

> The obligation to protect innocent individuals and society from harm overrides the prohibition against life-taking. We are obliged to defend the innocent if we are able to do so. Killing an aggressor becomes a morally acceptable possibility if it is done to protect the innocent from harm. Pacifists fail in their moral obligation toward innocent persons and society.[29]

---

29. Philosopher Jan Narveson has argued that the pacifist's refusal to violate the prohibition against life-taking is inconsistent. See "Pacifism, a Philosophical Analysis," in R.A. Wasserstrom, ed. *War and Morality* (Belmont, CA: Wadsworth, 1970). Narveson's argument is as follows. The defense against violence is a right and if one fails to protect that right, one unwittingly is morally as culpable as those who are violating that right in the first place by their acts of violence. Narveson accuses pacifists of a contradiction: they believe that violence violates the right not to be harmed but are unwilling to defend that right. But Narveson's argument is flawed. After beginning with the proposition that no innocent person should be subjected to violence, Narveson then makes violence a duty. For an excellent refutation of his position, see Jenny Teichman, *Pacifism and Just War: A Study in Applied Philosophy* (London: Basil Blackwell, 1986).

The pacifist:

> We agree that we must attempt to prevent harm to innocent persons, but it is the means of preventing harm that is of fundamental moral concern. We refuse to defend fellow citizens by intentionally killing other human beings. The prohibition against killing is universal and is not overridden by the obligation to protect the innocent. The prohibition applies to all, making it wrong for aggressors to attack innocent persons and nations, and wrong for defenders to kill in the nation's defense. The burden lies with non-pacifists to justify why the prohibition against killing should be overridden.

The prohibition against killing innocent persons is foundational for both positions. The pacifist is on solid ground to insist that a negative moral duty (the prohibition against harming) takes priority over a positive one (preventing someone from being harmed). It is important to bear in mind that although the just-war position sees the positive duty as sometimes overcoming the negative duty, the tradition has always been unequivocal in its prohibition against harming civilians. Simply put, civilians may not be directly attacked. Only soldiers can be directly disabled or killed — and treatment of soldiers is subject to the condition of "tactical proportionality."

However the positions may differ, they share a common starting point: the prohibition against doing harm and especially against life-taking. While this is obviously bedrock for pacifists, we must remember that the original just-war question, *whether* the prohibition of killing can ever be overridden, contains within it a strong presumption against life-taking.

The Catholic tradition on life-taking is very restrictive. As we have already noted, St. Augustine taught that it was necessary to subdue the barbarians and permissible to kill them in the process. Yet Augustine carefully qualified the morality of killing another human being. While Christians might kill in defense of others, he did *not* believe that they ought to kill *in their own defense*. Thus, Augustine permitted killing in defense of others but *not* of oneself (without confronting the logical difficulty of not permitting an agent the self-defense that might be necessary in order to engage in the defense of others). It was only later that the tradition permitted killing in self-defense. One finds St. Thomas teaching that it is morally permissible to kill in self-defense, provided that the deadly force is *intended only to preserve one's own life* and not to cause the death of the attacker. Thomas followed Augustine by permitting the taking of life in wartime, but he also taught that it was permitted to kill an assailant in self-defense provided that one *intended only self-defense* and that the death of the assailant was unintentional. Thomas applied the principle of double effect to make this distinction between intentional and unintentional (but foreseen) killing in circumstances of self-defense.[30] Thus, since Thomas, the tradition has permitted killing in wartime and in self-defense.[31]

However, later Catholic moralists have attempted to apply Thomas's principle of double effect to other situations, including the killing of noncombatants in wartime. It is important at this point in the Catholic tradition to be clear about what kinds of exceptional killing the tradition allowed. Augustine believed it was permissible for a Christian to kill an enemy soldier. Thomas believed it was also permissible to kill a personal attacker if the latter's death was unintended. Like Augustine, Thomas believed one could kill an enemy soldier, provided the war was justifiable in the first place. But neither of them taught that it was ever justifiable to kill noncombatants. Any discussion of the differences between pacifism and just-war on the matter of killing should be clear that the in-

---

30. Thomas Aquinas, *Summa Theologiae*, 2a2ae, Q. 64, art. 7. The principle of double effect requires that four criteria be observed: the immediate action must be morally good or indifferent; the foreseen evil effect must not intended in itself; the evil that is generated may not be a means to the good sought; and the good intended must be proportionate to the evil foreseen.

31. Thomas attempted to justify one other exception, that of capital punishment, but his argument (that criminal behavior results in the loss of full humanity) has long since been rejected by the Church.

junction against killing noncombatants has never been in dispute. It is simply unequivocally prohibited.

The pacifist conviction that killing in wartime is morally wrong is often challenged by presenting a scenario in which it appears counter-intuitive to hold that killing is always wrong. The pacifist is challenged with this question: Are you saying that you would not intervene to prevent an attack on an innocent person (e.g., your spouse/child/sister)? The question rightly assumes our natural inclination to defend ourselves and others. It also presumes that the only option available is the use of lethal force. Pacifists appear to be caught here: (1) those who would intervene are charged with inconsistency for intervening in the personal scenario while refusing to justify similar intervention in the larger, social arena; (2) at the same time, those who would *not* intervene are maligned as cowards, even to a criminal degree.

The pacifist's best response would be to question how close the analogy really is between killing in wartime and killing in defense of others (or self) in a civilian setting. Pacifists are opposed to the institution of war, which is a unique form of organized violence rather than merely a larger-scale version of protecting others from personal assault. The objective of war is to kill those on the enemy side. Soldiers, unlike citizens who may suddenly be asked to intervene, are trained to kill others and to follow orders to do so. Military training desensitizes men (and women) to overcome the normal taboo against killing, supplanting qualities such as compassion and respect with aggressiveness and the pretense of not being afraid. In wartime, killing is not one among a number of ways of resolving a crisis. It is the only way. Strategies for assaulting and killing the enemy are carefully planned. Assailants do not lunge from a darkened alley: they are trained by both sides. By contrast, in situations of defense against a personal attacker, the defender's *objective* is not to kill, even if that is the outcome. Unlike a battle scene, a personal attack scenario still contains the possibility for negotiating a nonviolent outcome and avoiding deadly harm to anyone.

In wartime, soldiers on both sides are assailants, posing real threats to one another. Normal categories of "innocent" versus "unjust" take on a new logic in wartime. "Innocents" include the vast majority of civilians on both sides (including the aggressor side). However, warmaking turns whole societies into "enemies." It locks thousands in its lethal embrace, leaving wholesale carnage in its wake, and poisoning the ground of future relations. Soldiers who are life-threatening to each other are "unjust." Yet they do not act on their own but on behalf of other peoples' political objectives. They have been recruited, some willingly and others unwillingly. In battle they are motivated by self-preservation as much as by the desire to kill. They are not innocent in the same manner that civilians are; but neither are they like the unprovoked attacker who lunges from the darkened alley. For these reasons, battlefields and theaters of war are not comparable to situations of sudden and unprovoked attack.

Thus, the pacifist is right to protest that intervening to prevent a personal assault bears little resemblance to prosecuting a war. The complex forces that lead to war, the mutual fear that drives soldiers to kill, and the lack of any other alternative to deadly force make war and the defense of innocents under unjust attack very different moral situations.[32] The circumstances that lead to war are usually complicated. Seldom is it a matter of an unprovoked attack.

In the pacifist perspective, the category of "enemy" is problematical because of religious teachings that regard enemies as neighbors who are to be loved. Pacifism recognizes the obligation to reform evildoers and to transform them into friends. Christian pacifists refuse to kill "enemies" and are, indeed, critical of the very category of "enemy." "Enemies" are only such because we have designated them as such. Beneath that label they, like us, are children of God. Their correct label is "neighbor-to-be-loved."

---

32. I am indebted to the article by John Howard Yoder, "What Would You Do If . . . ?" in *Journal of Religious Ethics* 2/2 (1974), 81-105.

To love one's neighbor is a demanding call, made even more demanding by the witness of Jesus. Christian pacifists believe that as followers of Jesus we must be courageous enough to suffer harm rather than resort to harming others when nonviolent strategies fail. (Users of violent strategies may be just as likely to suffer harm, though they may hope that their strategies will protect them). The pacifist understands suffering that is willingly undertaken as participation in the suffering love of Jesus, a love that is redemptive for all and capable of transforming enemies into friends. While both pacifist and just-war positions may be construed as a willingness to "lay down one's life" for friends in need, only the pacifist explicitly accepts being killed rather than killing as entailed in the meaning of self-sacrifice. The life of Jesus verifies the pacifist's rejection of violence as a means of disarming aggressors and resisting injustice. It gives them confidence in the transformative power of suffering-love. The resurrection attests to the ultimate power of nonviolent love.

Christian pacifism, writes theologian Lisa Cahill, is concerned about "the quality of a communal life grounded in Christ and in the Kingdom of God, a life that turns out to make violence incomprehensible" and that "emerges from a close-knit and converted way of life . . . [as] an outgrowth of discipleship. . . ."[33] Indeed, in his study of just-war and pacifist strands of Christianity, James Johnson argues that pacifism does not thrive outside of small groups of fellow believers. He has in mind various religious sectarian communities that have withdrawn from the wider society, removing themselves from the state and its violence. However, none of the groups that Johnson studies are Roman Catholic. While in some instances modern Catholic pacifism shares strong withdrawalist views of the state, most Catholic pacifists manifest a passion for justice and are far from politically uninvolved. Johnson observes that throughout Western history pacifism has been "tolerated as a spiritual conviction but not as a political statement," and that,

33. Lisa Sowle Cahill, *Love Your Enemies* (Minneapolis: Augsburg Fortress Press, 1994), 229.

in times of war, pacifists "stand out in stark contrast . . . be-com[ing] less able to make their pacifist voice heard . . . ."[34]

Johnson is touching on an effect of the secularism of modern life, the fact that use of religious language and the demonstration of religious belief in public is viewed with suspicion. Only religious convictions of the vaguest sort are tolerated in the public realm. Social criticisms offered in conspicuously religious forms are deemed sectarian ideas inappropriate in public conversation because of separation of church and state.

Johnson looks to just-war theory, by contrast, to provide us with a common language with which to engage in public discourse about war.[35] However, when we seek a common language that will offend no one, we may end up speaking unpersuasively to everyone. Indeed, if we are not ashamed of our faith we will seek to live a converted way of life in public.

Conclusion

The pacifism we have considered in this chapter has been abstract and disembodied: we have not examined the diversity of actual contemporary Catholic pacifists who have given pow-

---

34. Johnson, *The Quest for Peace*, 230, 232.

35. But when it led to pacifist conclusions during the Vietnam War, just-war reasoning was construed to be a religious moral theory. President Johnson established a commission to consider whether draftees could apply for conscientious objector status if they judged the war to be unjustifiable on just-war grounds. The majority opinion of the Commission advised that selective conscientious objection (SCO) should not be permitted, giving four reasons: (1) just-war teaching as "a classical Christian doctrine" is "not a matter upon which the Commission could pass judgment"; (2) support or nonsupport of the [Vietnam] war is a political issue; (3) recognition of SCO might lead to a generalized disrespect for law and refusal to perform the duties of citizenship; (4) it would be burdensome for those already in the military to make moral judgments about the war when it was "the government's obligation to make it for [them]. . . ." See *In Pursuit of Equity: Who Serves When Not All Serve?* Majority Report of the National Advisory Commission on Selective Service, Burke Marshall, Chairman (Washington, D.C.: U.S. Government Printing Office, 1967), 9. In the minds of the majority of the Commission, the just-war doctrine was a religious doctrine that did not have a place in public policy.

erful witness both to their fellow Catholics and to many others. We could have studied Dorothy Day and other members of the Catholic Worker Movement, Daniel and Philip Berrigan and other Catholic protestors against the Vietnam War and the nuclear arms race. Or we could have examined the thought of pacifist Gordon Zahn.[36] A pluralism of views can be found among Catholic pacifists. Often their views have not been developed with systematic rigor. All of these pacifists want to counter the fascination of war with a realism about the injustices it perpetuates rather than remedies. Protestors such as Day and the Berrigans have taken an "anti-worldly" stand, not against the world as such but against the powerful and privileged who produce armaments and neglect the poor. Their pacifism is not "other-worldly" but is motivated by a concern for justice. They are passionately critical of the idols of nationalism and weaponry. Their agenda has been to respond to the Gospel call to be peacemakers. True to the transformationist motif of Catholicism, they are committed to the capacity of Christian love to overcome animosities and bring about reconciliation.

Pacifists vary considerably, both in their world-view and in their practical commitments. For example, Gordon Zahn advocates the development of nonviolent methods of national defense. Daniel Berrigan engages in protest against the idolatrous features of American life in order to shake citizens out of their uncritical acceptance of the status quo. He is not concerned with developing alternative methods of defense. Some pacifists engage in acts of civil disobedience while others do not. Those who do may have different purposes: some may see civil disobedience as an effective method for bringing about social change while others see it as having more symbolic value. Pacifism stands as a continuous reminder to Christians that war must be kept on the outer edges of their way of life. Paci-

---

36. For surveys of twentieth-century Catholic pacifism, especially in the U.S., see Miller, Ch. 3, Musto, Ch. 15, and Patricia McNeal, *The American Catholic Peace Movement, 1928-1972* (1978) and *Harder Than War: Catholic Peacemaking in Twentieth Century America* (1992).

fism attempts to stretch our moral imaginations in order that
we may be able to discover nonviolent ways of attaining justice and peace. It also challenges the claim of the state to exercise the power of life and death.[37]

Catholic pacifism in our time is more aptly described as
"nonviolent resistance." Its function is to sensitize Christian
communities and commit them to peacemaking. Pacifism also
insists on the responsibilities of citizenship to defend the rights
of individuals and communities.[38] The growing number of
Catholic and Protestant Christians who have joined in nonviolent resistance against unjust and violent political structures refutes the charge that pacifism is socially irresponsible. Though
stereotypes of pacifism remain, perhaps making it necessary to
retire the word, burgeoning forms of nonviolent resistance
have given pacifism a new shape in the twentieth century.

While in their 1983 pastoral letter the U.S. Catholic Bishops briefly praised nonviolent resistance, they gave no more
than a passing glance at its contemporary practice. In the next
chapter, we will see how some Christian communities have
turned nonviolent commitments into effective political action.
These efforts stand in contrast to the ineffectiveness with
which anti-war groups in the U.S. responded to the circumstances that led to the war against Iraq. As we shall see, it is
simply false to hold that pacifists/nonviolent resisters are
without practical and effective political agendas. The stories in
the following chapter are but a few of the many instances of
contemporary Christians involved in nonviolent struggles.
They illustrate the political effectiveness of pacifism that
Johnson finds so lacking in earlier periods. Catholics in Poland
and the Philippines and Protestants in East Germany and
France have engaged in various forms of nonviolent resistance
against unjust and violent political regimes. Their actions re-

---

37. See Miller, 121-124.

38. Miller, however, is still not convinced that the U.S. Catholic Bishops'
endorsement of nonviolent resistance sufficiently addresses the specific duties
of pacifists regarding the defense of rights, especially "within a community
engaged in legitimate self-defense." *Interpretations in Conflict*, 36.

fute the charge that pacifism cannot bear fruit in organized and effective political action of a nonviolent nature.

Questions for Reflection

1. In what ways is the basis of pacifism among modern Christians different from that of the pacifism that existed in early Christianity?

2. In what ways are the teaching and example of Jesus relevant to pacifism? Are there any ways in which the New Testament is not applicable to moral assessment of war?

3. In what respects is the analogy between serving in a war and defending a neighbor from attack a "false analogy"?

4. Why do you think pacifism carries such negative connotations?

5. Describe the common ground between pacifism and just-war commitments.

6. What is "just-war pacifism"? Should selective conscientious objection be a legal right? Why or why not?

CHAPTER SEVEN

Christian Nonviolent Resistance

Introduction

I have noted earlier the long-standing Christian view, reflected in Augustine, that war is inevitable as a consequence of
human sinfulness and sometimes as a remedy for it. But other
Christian theologians have asserted that war is a failure of the
human imagination to discover alternatives to violence. In
their view, when war is no longer regarded as an *exceptional*
practice but as "business as usual," Christian communities
miss opportunities to become effective negotiators and to work
for reconciliation and peace.

When we are unable to imagine alternatives other than
war, our capacity for peacemaking is equally limited; for example, the terms for peace that the "winners" impose on the "los-
ers" are often notoriously inadequate to secure a stable peace.
Richard Miller concludes his discussion of just-war and pacifist
strands of Christianity by appealing to the need for expanded
moral imaginations. He writes:

> . . . granting that war is an extraordinary affair, stand-
> ing on the limits of our moral experience, it follows
> that much of our fascination with war and the dilem-
> mas of war ought to be removed from the center and
> placed at the periphery of our moral imaginations. If
> just-war ideas are designed to address the exceptional

case of national or international conflict, then it seems that in the normal (rather than the exceptional) course of human commerce we should work more assiduously to make the requirements of peace central to moral discourse and practice. . . . It seems entirely coherent for the just-war theorist, no less than for the pacifist, to develop positive requirements of peace for the ordinary course of human affairs. Placing just-war ideas at the edge of our moral imaginations ought to create a clearing in which the requirements of peace can be pursued with a wider range of conceptual and practical strategies than those available in an ethos dominated by a fascination with war. . . . Such exclusive attention to the dilemmas of war represents a myopic focus, one which misperceives the place of just-war ideas and eclipses considerations of the positive requirements of peace.[1]

Any discussion of Christian pacifism is inadequate that does not attend to the theory and practice of nonviolent resistance, the programmatic effort to resist injustice and defuse violence without adopting the violent methods of the adversary. This chapter will examine nonviolent resistance as it has been understood and practiced by contemporary Christian communities. A truly thorough study of nonviolent resistance would require examining the monumental influence of Mahatma Gandhi upon twentieth-century nonviolence and the nonviolent struggle for civil rights led by Martin Luther King, Jr. Here we will only refer in passing to the very large contribution of these apostles of nonviolence toward shaping a contemporary understanding and practice of nonviolent resistance.[2]

---

1. Miller, *Interpretations of Conflict*, 122.

2. Gandhi studies are voluminous. For an excellent study of his major ideas and an analysis of all of his major nonviolent campaigns in India, see Joan Bonderant, *The Conquest of Violence: The Gandhian Philosophy of Conflict* (1967). For an excellent account of King's nonviolence, see John Ansbro, *Martin Luther King: The Making of a Mind* (1982).

"Nonviolent resistance" was the phrase Gandhi used to describe the means by which his spiritual and political program of "satyagraha" was to be carried out. Inspired by Gandhi's ability to forge the demand of love of neighbor into a social program, Martin Luther King, Jr., made nonviolent resistance his creed and strategy for "saving the soul of America" by securing civil rights for its black citizens. In the following pages we will see the legacy of King and Gandhi in movements striving to defend oppressed peoples, dismantle or reform oppressive political systems, and achieve reconciliation with opponents. Especially significant for our purposes is the fact that all three movements of nonviolent resistance were supported and nurtured by the churches.

Robert Holmes describes the logic of nonviolent resistance this way:

> Viewed in one light, nonviolent action — particularly concerted action by large numbers of people — is simply the exercise of power. It is power that employs different means than are involved in the use of force. Rather than trying to prevail by marshalling greater force than one's opponent, its seeks to undermine the basis of an opponent's power. Governments, armies, occupying forces and institutions of any sort that control and regulate people's lives require the cooperation, or at least the acquiescence, of large numbers of people. Withdraw that cooperation and the foundations of such power crumble. Nonviolence studies techniques by which to do that. These techniques require studying with as much care as traditionally has gone into study of violence and warfare.[3]

Gene Sharp extensively studied the techniques of nonviolent resistance (or "civilian-based defense," as he tends to call it).[4]

---

3. Robert Holmes, "The Morality of Nonviolence" in *Just War, Nonviolence and Nuclear Deterrence*, Duane Cady and Richard Werner, eds. (Wakefield, New Hampshire: Longwood Academic, 1991), 131-132.

4. See especially Gene Sharp, *The Politics of Nonviolent Action* (1973), *Social Power and Political Freedom* (1980), and *National Security Through Civilian-Based Defense* (1985).

These techniques have been (and are being) used by people of many religious and political persuasions throughout the world and are often the basis for interfaith and secular discussions of peacemaking.

This chapter will examine several instances of nonviolent resistance undertaken by Christian communities in the past two decades in order to see how they joined faith to nonviolent political action. In the course of telling the stories of twentieth-century nonviolent resistance we will see some of its successful techniques. We will also see its connection to Christian faith.

The accounts of nonviolent resistance offered in this chapter might serve as clearings amidst "an ethos dominated by a fascination with war" in which we might perceive "the positive requirements of peace." Two movements occurred in Poland and East Germany as first steps in casting off the oppressive yoke of Communism. The third account is that of the nonviolent overthrow of the Marcos regime in the Philippines. The chapter concludes by considering the lessons of these movements.

1. Poland

The plague of Nazism had barely subsided when Stalinism descended over Eastern Europe, dashing the hopes of peoples who had suffered grievously under Hitler to reclaim their freedom and rebuild their societies. In Eastern Europe, the germination and first flowering of nonviolent resistance as a means of social change took place in Poland. Its success there gave other oppressed peoples courage to overcome their fear and to struggle for change without resort to counterviolence. Three decades of Polish human rights struggle and commitment to nonviolence has played a catalytic role in the liberation of Eastern Europe. The toppling of the Berlin Wall in 1989 was the dramatic culmination of largely peaceful protests throughout the 1980s. These astonishing upheavals were the fruit of a spiritual process nurtured by the churches. Through prayer, social critique, and self-disciplined protest, religious communities helped to bring about social change .

Assuming full power in 1949, the Marxist-Leninist regime of Poland had sought to eliminate all rivals for the loyalty of the Polish people. By 1950, the Catholic Church remained the only organized opposition to Poland's rule by the Communist Party. By 1952, eight bishops and over nine hundred priests were in prison. In 1953 Cardinal Stefan Wyszynski, Archbishop of Warsaw and head of the Church in Poland was declared an enemy of the socialist revolution and jailed. The imprisoned clergy symbolized the captive nation.

In his prison diary, Wyszynski identified Poland's suffering with that of Christ, urged forgiveness, and countered the state doctrine of hatred with love. Out of that suffering new spiritual strength was gathered to oppose the social construction being imposed on Poland. After release from prison in 1956, Cardinal Wyszynski proclaimed a nine year period of spiritual renewal in preparation for the 1966 celebration of the millennium of Polish Christianity. Since the mid-1950s, the Church's "Light and Life" movement to evangelize the youth of Poland had been growing. In 1961, the Communist regime suppressed all religious education.

Wyszynski responded defiantly: "If a citizen does not demand his rights, he is no longer a citizen but a slave."[5] What citizenship demanded, he declared, was to throw off the yoke by means of "heroic sacrifices and massive shocks to bring about the awakening of the man who no longer fights for his freedom . . . and of the nation which no longer fulfills its obligations in the name of its most important and sacred right — its freedom."[6] The regime was unable to silence the Church as it stood up for human dignity and defended the right of conscience. In effect, it had become the only institution left in Poland where the truth could be spoken.

---

5. Quoted in Mary Craig, *Lech Walesa and His Poland* (New York: Continuum, 1987), 114.

6. Craig, 125.

Beneath the bleakness of Polish life, a ferment of spiritual renewal and an alternative social reconstruction was underway. The Church promoted a radically different social vision. Against the state dogma of the necessity of class conflict and of hatred toward all who impeded the rise of the socialist state, it preached the necessity of love and forgiveness. Giving witness to its teachings, the Polish bishops in 1965 sent a letter to the German Catholic bishops seeking reconciliation and friendship to end the heritage of Polish-German animosity and suspicion. The regime was outraged: its strategy for Polish unity had been to perpetuate distrust of Germany. In retaliation, the regime denied the Bishops passports to attend the final sessions of the Second Vatican Council in Rome. The historian Bohdan Cywinski describes how the Church gave people courage during those years:

> People began to understand that they could gather in large numbers for religious purposes and no harm would come to them. They learned to keep calm, and to carry on praying or doing whatever they had to do. . . . It was an apprenticeship — a lesson that even under a hostile regime you can achieve something without violence.[7]

The "heroic sacrifices and massive shocks" which Wyszynski prescribed for Polish society were not to take the form of retaliatory violence against the already pervasive violence of the regime. Reconstruction of the society would mean first of all overcoming fear and resisting retaliation against the guardians of this bleak and brutal society. The Church proclaimed the power of nonviolent Christian love in a repressive environment. It helped to educate the people in alternative forms of political participation (avoiding confrontation with security forces, riot police, and the Soviet troops waiting across the border).

The Church's message had its most powerful leavening effect in Poland's industrial work-places where workers began

---

7. Craig, 125.

to protest food shortages and to demand a voice in the reform of the Polish economy. In December 1970, Poland's shipyard workers in Gdansk on the Baltic coast staged a strike and demanded the establishment of trade unions independent of the regime. The strikers moved from the shipyard to the streets of Gdansk where a large and violent crowd surrounded and stormed the central Gdansk police headquarters. Authorities declared a state of emergency and cut off all communication into and out of the coastal region. Several hours later, unaware that Gdansk authorities had ordered the shipyard closed, hundreds of workers attempted to report for work. State troops opened fire on workers as they emerged from the rail station on their way to the shipyard. The government hastily buried the dead in unmarked graves. No one doubted that the official death toll of 26 was only a fraction of the actual number.

Lech Walesa was among the leaders of the Gdansk strike. He could not forget the violence of December 1970, and demanded a monument to the fallen workers. He also saw the potential for more violence after years of deprivation and repression and the sudden prospect of change. The lesson of nonviolence was being learned painfully. He wanted no more spilled blood and split skulls, requiring more monuments. Walesa counseled patience, forbearance, and self-discipline among workers. He urged them not to seek vengeance against the regime and its supporters, declaring: "The point is not to smash your head open in one day, but to win, step by step, without offending anyone."[8] Walesa fearlessly accused the regime of assaulting the dignity of the Polish people and demanded reform. As one observer writes, Walesa "used words honestly, and gave them a truthfulness that years of doublespeak had taken from them."[9] While Walesa was unwavering in his demands on behalf of workers, he also professed, "I am a believer, which is why I forgive blindly. I can be having a real go at someone, and then all at once I see standing oppo-

---

8. Craig, 204.

9. Craig, 182.

site me another human being."[10] Walesa preached the overcoming of violence by conquering one's own fear and renouncing the use of counter-violence. He was dismissed from his job at the shipyard in 1976 for his organizing activities.

As the U.S. was celebrating its bicentennial in 1976, Jacek Kuron and Adam Michnik were founding the "Committee for the Defense of Workers" (KOR), comprised of progressive professionals, scientists, and artists demanding democratization of Polish socialism. Kuron and Michnik advocated nonviolent methods for liberating Polish society. Assessing the dangers and the opportunities present in the ongoing national crisis and reflecting on the massacre of shipyard workers in 1970, Kuron wrote:

> The anti-reform policy of the Polish state leadership always contains the danger of popular explosion. The only possibility afforded to the population to ward off this danger is that of self-organization. Only by peaceful methods, like peaceful demonstrations that do not disturb public order, only by means of stubborn negotiations with the state power, can the population strive for the successful attainment of its political will and force the state power to accept its wishes for reform.[11]

KOR received the support of the Catholic Church and was bolstered by Pope John Paul II's visit to Poland in 1979.

In August of 1980 another strike broke out at the Gdansk shipyard and quickly spread throughout the region and eventually into over 400 factories throughout the country. Led by a strike committee that included Walesa, several thousand workers occupied the shipyard. Walesa vowed:

> We will not abandon the shipyards and we will not give the militia any reason for intervening. Should they try to break up the strike before it winds up, we will not do anything against them. We don't struggle, we won't get into fights; we will merely sit down and drag

10. Craig, 193.

11. Quoted in Rainer Hildebrandt, *From Gandhi to Walesa* (Berlin: Verlag Hausam Checkpoint Charlie, 1987), 146.

the peace. They can come in and carry us away, all sixteen thousand of us, one by one.[12]

The workers did not take to the streets or engage in any acts of violence against the government. The citizens of Gdansk brought the strikers food, lifting it over the shipyard fences. Priests entered the shipyard to celebrate Mass with them. So committed were the strikers to avoiding violent behavior that a ban on alcohol was effectively observed by strikers throughout the region. After two weeks, the government agreed to the list of 21 worker demands, including free and independent trade unions.[13] The "Solidarity" movement was born and a social revolution was underway. Throughout the fall of 1980, tensions remained high. The Soviet Union threatened to deploy troops. In December, Pope John Paul II wrote to Soviet leader Leonid Brezhnev, advising him that Poland must manage its own internal affairs and that the Church could play a mediating and moderating role. Solidarity leaders did not call for the seizure of political power or for the rejection of socialism. Instead of fueling antagonism against the Communist Party, Solidarity's revolution aimed at solving massive economic and social problems and at reuniting Polish society by overcoming years of pervasive fear and distrust. A joint Church and government commission was established which declared that national unity was a priority "regardless of the differences in world outlook or political views."[14] The Church continued to set a conciliatory tone with the Bishops calling for the abandoning of hatred and the rebuilding of mutual trust. Cardinal Jozef Glemp, Wyszynski's successor, wrote to the people: "Let us look at ourselves truthfully. We shall see our own sins . . . and this will allow us to see the good done by the other side."[15]

---

12. Quoted in Hildebrand, 151.

13. For a full list of the demands, see Jean-Yves Potel, *The Promise of Solidarity* (New York: Praeger Publishers, 1982), 219-220.

14. Craig, 195.

15. Craig, 214.

When Solidarity was barely a year old, the regime moved against it. In December 1981, General Wojciech Jaruzelski, Prime Minister of the regime, declared a "state of war." A woman who heard the announcement from a Warsaw taxi inquired wearily and in disbelief: who had invaded Poland now? The driver explained and she understood only too well: in an ironic twist of the Marxist-Leninist war against the bourgeoisie, Jaruzelski had declared war on Solidarity, now ten million members strong. His imposition of martial law dispensed with the nascent freedoms the people had won a year earlier. Solidarity was banned and Walesa, Michnick and scores of Solidarity and KOR leaders were jailed. For the Polish people and their new confidence to confront the regime unarmed, Jaruzulski's "war" produced another siege of suffering. Yet it was not their darkest hour, only the hour before dawn. Again, the Church raised the sole voice of opposition. Cardinal Glemp responded to the imposition of martial law with a plea for nonviolence: "The most important thing is to avoid bloodshed. There is nothing of greater value than human life."[16] The Polish Bishops' conference called on the regime to restore civil rights, to release all political prisoners, and to renew its dialogue with Solidarity. The Church itself assisted workers who had been fired and imprisoned and provided aid to their families.

The Solidarity movement eventually outlasted Jaruzelski and the Polish Communist Party. Embroiled in its own domestic and foreign policy failures, Moscow instructed Warsaw to handle its own domestic troubles. Jaruzelski's war against Polish workers and peasants failed because it had come up against something more powerful than armed resistance. His military threats had not intimidated the force of human spirit which stood firmly against him. The victors would eventually be the Polish people, workers and intellectuals, many of them sons and daughters of the Catholic Church, who had joined in common cause with those who did not share their faith.

---

16. Craig, 234.

In 1983, Solidarity leaders were released from prison and Walesa was awarded the Nobel Peace Prize. The Nobel Committee wrote:

> Lech Walesa's activities were marked by a determination to solve the problems of his country by discussions and cooperation without force. He managed to make possible the dialogue between the organization "Solidarity" and the authorities. The Committee regarded Walesa as an exponent of the active longing for peace and freedom. . . . At a time when the easing of tensions and the peaceful resolution of conflicts are more important than at any other time . . . [his] initiative is an inspiration and an example.[17]

In his acceptance, Walesa declared: "we can effectively oppose violence only if we do not resort to it. . . . We will defend our rights but will not allow ourselves to be overcome by hatred. . . . "[18] Walesa reflected Poland's quest for freedom. The regime's attempt to intimidate him and destroy Solidarity failed on account of the inner freedom the people had acquired. Supported first by the Catholic Church and later by the workers movement, the Polish people acquired a spiritual weapon of great magnitude: the power to overcome fear and seek reconciliation with opponents.

The story of Poland and Solidarity is the story of a courageous, patient, and nonviolent quest for social justice and peace. It had its martyrs, including Fr. Jerzy Popieluszko, murdered by the regime in 1984. Eulogizing Popieluszko, Walesa said:

> They wanted to kill, and they wanted not only a man, not only a Pole, not only a priest. They wanted to kill the hope that it is possible in Poland to avoid violence in political life.[19]

---

17. Quoted in Hildebrand, 142.
18. Craig, 271.
19. *Time* (November 12, 1984), 58.

The story is about a spiritual process in which the Polish church and people effected a social transformation through the power of love. It is the story of the Gospel of love carried into politics by numerous courageous Poles. Walesa and the millions who joined the Solidarity movement bore witness to the convictions of Gandhi and King, that nonviolent resistance is a force more potent than military force. Poland's liberation spilled across borders, inspiring people in other Soviet bloc countries to speak out against the abuses of their respective regimes.

2. East Germany, 1981-1989

In East Germany the practices of nonviolent resistance produced a victory in 1989 with the overthrow of the communist regime and the tearing down of the Berlin Wall.

The Protestant churches of East Germany played a central role in those events. For 45 years the Communist regime had marginalized those who had attempted to practice their faith. But, as in Poland, the Party was unable to silence the East German church. There, too, the churches were the only effective opposition to the repressive state, becoming, in the words of Helmar Junghans, a Lutheran pastor and Leipzig University professor of church history, "the shield against Communist attack, the shelter of action groups, the champion of the reforms and the voice of nonviolence."[20]

In 1960, the "Friedensdekade" was initiated: ten days each November devoted to prayer that concluded with a day of repentance. In the early 1970s, the East German Government (German Democratic Republic) sought admission to the U.N. and increased trade with the West. Hoping to win international good will, it took measures to acknowledge the nation's cultural heritage, even permitting international celebrations of Martin Luther's 500th birthday. Junghans describes the various initiatives taken by the Protestant churches in this period of

---

20. Helmar Junghans, "The Christians' Contribution to the Non-violent Revolution in the GDR in the Fall of 1989," *Philosophy and Theology* 6,1 (Fall, 1991), 79-93, at 80.

slight thaw in GDR-Christian relations. One of those initiatives, conducted in Lutheran churches, was an "Education for Peace" program that sought to provide young people with a different worldview from the Party's teaching on the necessity of class violence. Increasingly, churches became the meeting places for study groups, places where both Christians and people not religious "learned to ask the Communist government questions to which they could scarcely give an answer."[21] Week-long workshops on peace were organized which provided information on issues and sought solutions. In Halle, East Germany, an annual, ecumenical "Bridge Worship" for justice and peace began in 1980. In 1981, Leipzig Protestant parishes began to meet in Nikolaikirche every Monday to pray for peace and for a reversal of plans to install intermediate-range missiles in Western and Eastern Europe. Although the missiles were deployed in 1983, the prayer groups continued to grow. In 1987, a conciliar process was underway in several East German cities consisting of meetings in churches to discuss social issues and the churches' role in dealing with them. These meetings often concluded with candle-lit processions through the various cities.

During this period, the churches had also worked with the GDR to negotiate permission for political dissidents to leave the country. Negotiations had usually been confidential because the atheist regime would not publicly do business with the churches. However, the churches' growing political activism had made public confrontation inevitable. In 1981, mass arrests were made of those who, in association with the "Friedensdekade," distributed and wore patches bearing an image of a sculpture entitled "Swords into Plowshares." With dissent in Poland now galvanized into the Solidarity movement, the apprehensive GDR leadership sought to suppress popular opposition. The government took aim at the Monday prayer services, arresting participants on the charges that such gatherings were intended to support dissidents seeking permission to emigrate. Environmental protests in mid-1980s brought more

---

21. Junghans, 81.

arrests and reprisals against parishioners by the Communist Party, and increased the risk that the government might deny the churches the freedom to carry out their pastoral tasks. The religious press continued to raise issues involving the environment, alternative national service, popular education, legal rights, mass media policies, expatriation and freedom of travel. The government, in turn, sought to limit circulation by withholding paper for printing.

In the summer of 1989, the confrontation between the GDR and the churches reached crisis proportions when the churches publicly demanded an investigation of fraud in the May elections. Arrests of those attending Monday prayer services continued to grow. In October, the synod of the Union of Protestant Churches protested that "young people who demonstrate in a nonviolent fashion are oppressed through violence; participants are punished unjustly. . . ."[22] Junghans notes the estrangement of the East German Communist Party from the Gorbachev reforms and the result "that the tanks of the Red Army had not yet been available to the government of the GDR in the fall of 1989," and considers this to be "one of the decisive reasons why the confrontation between reformers and the government did not break out earlier."[23] The decisive confrontation in October of 1989 was incredible both for the absence of tanks and the nonviolent discipline of the thousands of anti-government demonstrators. Junghans describes the role of the churches in the dramatic collapse of the Honecker government and the Berlin Wall:

> More and more people began to participate in the peace prayers at the Nikolaikirche in Leipzig. Soon the church was no longer able to hold all of the people. Many thousands of them stood in the street around the church. The message was clear: The government had to act. Would it again use guns and tanks? . . . the hospitals of Leipzig had been prepared to admit a lot of wounded people. The situation was at a breaking

22. Junghans, 91.

23. Junghans, 89.

point. The voice of the church to abstain from violence was amplified to both sides.[24]

Junghans reports that Lutheran Bishop Johannes Hempel of Leipzig demanded talks between the government and demonstrators. As the Communist government rapidly lost popular support, the churches arranged talks between reformist groups and the government — in church facilities chaired by church officials. At the same time that Bishop Hempel called for talks, he also pleaded for calm among the demonstrators and for no use of violence under any circumstances. Others followed his lead. Thousands demonstrated nonviolently and police did not resort to arms against them. Describing these events, Jorg Swoboda has written: "Gorbachev's *perestroika* and *glasnost* had given the people courage. God had blessed them with unyielding patience and unconquerable nonviolence. They had overcome their fear and found their voice and self-respect again."[25] After experiencing repression and fear for four decades, the people experienced the truth of the Gospel: "Blessed are the meek, for they shall inherit the land." And the Berlin Wall, the symbol of oppression in that land, came tumbling down.

The story of European peace movements that helped bring an end to the Cold War is much broader than the two accounts provided here suggest. For instance, West Germans sought peace by resisting another kind of oppression: a nuclear deterrence strategy that made Germany the first line of defense in a U.S.-Soviet confrontation in Europe.[26] Besides Poland and

---

24. Junghans, 91.

25. Jorg Swoboda, *The Revolution of the Candles* (Wuppertal und Kassel: Oncken Verlag, 1990), 5.

26. The West German peace movement arose precisely out of the perception of the futility of a war in Europe, particularly a war involving the use of nuclear weapons. The protests on behalf of human rights in eastern Europe and on behalf of nuclear disarmament in West Germany drew on a variety of sources and attracted a variety of participants. Among the extensive literature on European peace movements, see *West European Pacifism and the Strategy for Peace*, Peter van den Dungen, ed. (New York: St. Martin's Press, 1985).

East Germany, popular movements just as massive and almost entirely nonviolent occurred in Hungary, Bulgaria, and Czechoslovakia. These movements toppled governments and initiated the painful processes of social reconstruction. For example, in August 1991, a large crowd shielded the Russian Parliament Building, with Boris Yeltsin and other elected officials within, from a military assault. Fr. Aleksandr Borisov, an Orthodox priest and Moscow city council member, distributed two thousand Bibles to soldiers and another two thousand to people on the barricades. Patriarch Alexis of the Russian Orthodox Church threatened that soldiers firing on the people would be excommunicated.[27]

What has been accomplished over the past decade in Europe cannot but change our thinking about nonviolence. There we witnessed the success of nonviolence on a large social scale. In both Eastern Europe and West Germany the churches played instrumental roles in the nonviolent movements which blossomed in the 1980s into nonviolent revolutions which brought down the Berlin Wall, toppled repressive communist regimes, and achieved the most significant steps toward disarmament since the onset of the arms race.

Glen Stassen refers to a "new paradigm" arising from the eastern European experience of the 1980s, involving a process by which " . . . people who have lived in the face of oppression, violation of their basic rights, and the nuclear threat, with political scientists, Christian ethicists, and activists fashioned realistic steps of peacemaking that enabled them to begin living in the time after the Cold War even before the Wall came down."[28] All across Europe many people began to realize that the use of violence would be self-defeating and, in the Eastern European contexts, that the counterviolence could result in massive suffering. It is often argued that the recent nonviolent revolutions in Europe had no choice but to be nonviolent. Indeed, Eastern European protestors were no military match for

---

27. See Timothy G. Ash, *We The People: The Revolution of Eighty-Nine.*

28. Glen Stassen, *Just Peacemaking*, 18.

their political regimes. But if that point is made to suggest that nonviolence is a "second best" option, the great popular strength forged by these movements leads to the opposite conclusion. That is, nonviolent resistance is a more powerful method for overcoming oppression. In its weakness lies its strength.

3. The Philippines: The Nonviolent Revolution of 1986

Ferdinand Marcos became president of the Philippines in 1965. Over the next two decades he consolidated his power through control of the economy and military. This consolidation allowed the Marcos family and its cronies to extract great wealth from the country and to crush political opposition. Marcos depicted his regime as a staunch defender against communist insurgency groups. He was the U.S.'s strongest ally in the Pacific. For assurances that its military bases would be secure in the Philippines, the U.S. offered Marcos friendship and financial assistance. But the corruption of the Marcos government — nowhere more evident than in the political machinations and sumptuous lifestyle of First Lady Imelda Marcos — gave rise to strong popular opposition. In 1972, Marcos declared martial law and arrested thousands of his opponents, including opposition leader, Benigno Aquino. Aquino was imprisoned until 1980 when he was allowed to go to the U.S. for heart surgery, where he remained until 1983. His return in August of 1983 lasted less than one minute: he was gunned-down on the tarmac of the Manila International Airport as he descended from his plane. The Marcos government denied responsibility, but the ruthlessness and lack of support for the regime led to a coalescence of opposition against Marcos led by Aquino's widow, Corazon Aquino.

The majority of the Catholic clergy and episcopacy in the Philippines were politically conservative and had been generally supportive of the Marcos government. Yet the changing attitude of the Church in the 1980s was embodied in Cardinal Jaime Sin, Archbishop of Manila since 1974, and head of the Catholic Church in the Philippines. The opposition came to find an increasingly powerful voice in the Cardinal who, in his eulogy at Benigno Aquino's funeral mass, blamed the Marcos regime "for creating an atmosphere of oppression and corruption." Sin pleaded for nonviolence amidst the growing tension between the regime and opposition groups: "Can man liberate man without recourse to violence? Our answer to that is an unequivocal Yes."[29] His words contrasted sharply with a communist slogan evident at Aquino's funeral: "no reconciliation under the fascist dictatorial regime."

In late 1985, Marcos announced that the 1987 Presidential elections would be moved up to February 1986 — a move calculated to demonstrate to his U.S. ally that he enjoyed popular support.

Cardinal Sin was to play a pivotal role in the election that would become the nonviolent revolution of 1986. Sin had been instrumental in the creation the National Citizens' Movement for Free Elections (NAMFREL), "a watchdog group that had marshalled half a million people in a vain attempt to ensure honest polls."[30] Many NAMFREL workers testified that they considered their movement to be a Christian lay apostolate. In December of 1985, Sin took the first step in unseating Marcos by persuading Salvador Laurel, the country's second most popular opposition leader, to accept the vice-presidential spot on Cory Aquino's presidential ticket. Without a united opposition, the resulting split-vote would have made Marcos's claim of a "mandate" easier. The Philippine Conference of Catholic Bishops met twice during the campaign and twice issued pastoral letters protesting the corruption within the Marcos camp. The week before the election, they warned that "these elections can become one great offense to God and a national scandal."[31] Their letter, which was read from most church pulpits and

---

29. Quoted in Lewis Simons, *Worth Dying For* (New York: William Morrow, 1987), 43.

30. Bryan Johnson, *The Four Days of Courage* (New York: The Free Press, 1987), 46.

31. Quoted by Johnson, 53.

which appeared as a full-page newspaper ad, detailed Marcos-era election fraud:

> vote-buying, bribery, unwarranted pressures, serious lies, black propaganda, the fraudulent casting, canvassing, and reporting of votes, snatching and switching of ballot boxes, physical violence and killing . . . [all] threatening to escalate to a level never before experienced.[32]

In the days immediately before the elections, Marcos forces were buying votes at a frantic pace — so widespread was it that Cardinal Sin issued a statement that Catholics must vote their conscience but that they could take Marcos bribes without any obligation to deliver their vote to Marcos. The Cardinal later explained his reasoning: ". . . the people were being bribed with their own money. They were poor, they needed it badly, and certain quarters were offering it. We said, 'Take it. It's yours. There's no sin in that. But if you change your vote . . . *then* you have sinned.'"[33]

The February 7, 1986 election was, by all accounts, the most fraudulent in Filipino history. Two days later, computer operators for the national election commission in Manila, who were still tallying votes, walked off their jobs charging massive evidence of fraud in vote reporting. Fearing reprisals against them, the operators were given refuge in a nearby Catholic church and later hidden at an undisclosed location. By February 11, Marcos was projected as the winner. On that morning, Cardinal Sin made a trip to the NAMFREL headquarters to rally hundreds of dejected NAMFREL volunteers, whom he exhorted to stay the course:

> I know you are doing your best to restore the freedom and dignity of the Filipino people. I know how much courage you have shown, and how much you have suffered in the recent elections. The Bible says much about the virtue of suffering . . . and you, you members of

---

32. Johnson, 53.
33. Johnson, 53.

NAMFREL, have shown me how to suffer. I am inspired by you, and sometimes I am ashamed. . . . Some
of you have died for your country, but now I ask you
to go forth and live for your country! . . . In you lies
the Spirit, and may the Lord bless you. We will abide
with you. We will support you to the very end. . . .
You cannot truly enjoy Easter Sunday unless you have
suffered the pain of Good Friday. This is our Good Friday, but Sunday is coming soon. Stay here and wait for
it. Don't leave us yet. You must stay and see the resurrection.[34]

Sin's words were interrupted with news of the assassination of
a popular former provincial governor and Aquino supporter.
The Cardinal appeared unshaken by the news, utterly confident that the resurrection of which he spoke was at hand.

Most observers of the Church's role in the elections
thought that Cardinal Sin had now mustered all his power and
had still come up short against the power of the desperate and
ruthless Marcos regime. Four days later, Marcos succeeded in
having himself declared the winner by the members of the national assembly who had not walked out in protest. But the
charges of fraud stuck. What the church did next not only
helped to make them stick but also denied the legitimacy of
the Marcos regime. The Philippine Catholic Conference of 108
bishops prepared another pastoral letter. The letter signalled a
break between the Catholic Church and the Marcos regime and
was published despite the intense efforts of Imelda Marcos to
stop it. After noting the widespread election fraud, the Bishops
drew this stunning conclusion: "These, and other irregularities,
point to the criminal use of power to thwart the sovereign will
of the people. . . . We are morally certain the people's real will
for change has been truly manifested."[35] Having declared that
"a government that assumes or retains power through fraudulent means has no moral basis," the Bishops offered two
options. The first was addressed to the Marcos government:

---

34. Quoted in Johnson, 49.
35. Johnson, 57.

recognize the people's will and relinquish power. If Marcos refused, the Bishops urged the people to engage in a "systematically organized . . . nonviolent struggle by means of active nonresistance [to] correct the evil that [the government] has inflicted. . . ."[36]

The opposition that brought about the revolution of 1986 included several key players. Corazon Aquino and her running mate, Salvador Laurel, had broad popular support — a fact the U.S. conceded (after the people had taken to the streets) by acknowledging that she had won the popular vote. The day after the Marcos-dominated National Assembly declared Marcos the winner, Aquino declared victory and called for civil disobedience against his regime and a nation-wide boycott of the economic enterprises controlled by the Marcos family and their cronies. The next day she produced a list of the enterprises. Marcos may have calculated that he could ride out a storm with Cardinal Sin (once referred to as "the only man in the country whom Marcos fears, the only man he'll listen to because he carries the full weight of the Roman Catholic Church"),[37] but he had not anticipated the Cardinal's direct appeal to the people and the "people power" that quickly materialized.

Other key players were not committed to a nonviolent overthrow of the Marcos regime. As Aquino announced her victory, Minister of Defense Juan Enrile, General Fidel Ramos and other military officers who joined them, plotted a coup that involved capturing Marcos and his family, killing his key military leaders, and establishing a provisional committee comprised of military officers and civilians to govern the country. Aquino knew about the plot during the last month of her campaign. She did not know when it would occur, nor had the conspirators offered her any assurance of support beyond including her in the provisional governing committee.

---

36. Johnson, 60.
37. Lewis, 94.

The coup was set for the night of February 23. But on February 22 Marcos's security forces discovered the plot and prepared to take action against Enrile and Ramos at the Ministry of Defense and the adjacent military camp. Enrile and Ramos pleaded for help from Cardinal Sin and the U.S. Ambassador, expecting at any moment the arrival of Marcos's forces from the Presidential Palace two miles away. But Marcos hesitated, and in the meantime the churches of Manila organized a human blockade of thousands of lay people, nuns and seminarians on the causeway down which Marcos's marines and their tanks finally came. The tanks slowed to a standstill in front of the sea of Filipinos celebrating the hour of national liberation; their drivers refused radio commands to proceed to the rebel encampment. As a critical day passed, almost all of Marcos's military forces defected. On February 25, he requested safe passage for his family out of the Philippines through the U.S. diplomatic mission.

A dictatorship dependent on a pervasive military presence had failed. Likewise, a military coup had failed. Loyalty to the Church (and to Corazon Aquino) and commitment to nonviolence had produced a "people power" capable of overthrowing a corrupt regime without the customary wave of retribution and vengeance against loyalists. Their lives having been saved, the rebels had no choice but to recognize Aquino's mandate. The people had won their first victory in two decades. At the heart of the victory was the nonviolent means by which it was accomplished.

Conclusion: The Lessons of Nonviolent Resistance

This chapter has focused on accounts of successful contemporary nonviolent resistance. What lessons may be drawn from them? In Poland and East Germany, nonviolent strategies prevented bloodshed and possible civil wars and social reconstruction was begun. It is highly doubtful that violent confrontation with the oppressive and corrupt regimes could have been as successful. In the Philippines, the confrontation between Marcos's forces and the opposition reached the brink of violence when thousands of people interposed themselves between the two sides. The victory for democracy and nonviolence was won by the Church's nonviolent preaching and mobilization of the people, perhaps assisted by Marcos's hesitation to move immediately against Enrile and Ramos.

Instead of seeking to wrestle political power away from those who held it in order to place it in the hands of an opposition group, protestors in each of these captive nations advocated economic and social reform and championed human rights. Solidarity's leadership reassured the regime that they did not seek to control the reins of government but instead wished to sit down and cooperatively work out solutions to Poland's problems. The point was not to deepen the chaos already fraying the social fabric. Of course, the political power of all three regimes continued to disintegrate by reason of their own failure to serve the people.

The churches played a critical role in these nonviolent revolutions. The churches condemned injustices and advocated radical reforms. Nonetheless, they did not allow themselves to be simply identified with the political opposition. The Catholic bishops of the Philippines came closest to being so identified by their direct influence on the Presidential elections of 1986, although it should be pointed out that they were opposing the corruption of the democratic process more than endorsing Cory Aquino. In Poland and East Germany the churches urged restraint on all sides and took conciliatory initiatives as crises mounted.

In East Germany the churches also played a crucial intermediary role in the transfer of power when the Honecker regime collapsed.

Particularly in Poland and in East Germany, nonviolent resistance was part of the process of spiritual renewal of churches severely tested by three decades of repression. The Polish church preached forgiveness of enemies — whether Communist Party functionaries or German neighbors — as a critical aspect of nonviolence. The Polish bishops also sought reconciliation by urging the people to acknowledge their own complicity in the failures of their society. In the late 1960s, for example, the bishops spoke out against the resurgence of anti-semitism in Polish society. Liturgies for peace and freedom helped to educate and sustain the laity in their nonviolent struggles. In all three societies, nonviolent movements were nurtured by the preaching of the Gospel. Filipino Bishop Francisco Claver wrote:

> We choose nonviolence . . . because we believe it is the way Christ himself struggled for justice. In short, we equate it with the very Gospel of Christ.[38]

The preaching of the churches nurtured nonviolent discipline among the laity who joined with others in nonviolent demonstrations at the grassroots level.

In Chapter Six, we noted that pacifist coalitions before the World Wars were not effective in preventing war and had quickly lost most of their support with the onset of war. Could nonviolent resistance be expected to suffer the same fate? One way to answer that question is to compare contemporary non-violent resistance with German Catholic pacifism during the rise of Nazism. Studies of Catholic pacifism in that era report that several bishops, who were at one point vocal advocates of pacifism, were equally supportive of the German war effort a few years later. Gordon Zahn offers the following explanation of the quick erosion of German Catholic pacifism.[39] Although the Church protested numerous Nazi policies, it strongly identified itself with German society and the state and was strongly anti-Bolshevik. In addition, during Hitler's rise to power the German Catholic laity had no tradition of individual dissent and protest with which to resist Nazism. As a result, the pacifism espoused by members of the hierarchy quickly evaporated as church leaders and laity succumbed to nationalism and patriotism. Hence, as a voice of opposition, the Church was ineffective. In the end, the chief Catholic witness

---

38. Bishop Francisco Claver, *Fellowship* (June, 1985).

39. Gordon Zahn, *German Catholics and Hitler's War: A Study in Social Control* (New York: Sheed and Ward, 1962).

consisted of a handful of Catholics who resisted Hitler and were martyred.

The contemporary churches of Poland, East Germany, and the Philippines had not aligned themselves as closely with the secular power structure but had been able to maintain a critical distance — in the case of Poland and East Germany, there was little choice! In addition, they championed the laity in their bid for greater political self-determination. In all, the churches contributed to a less narrowly nationalistic politics and encouraged the taking of personal responsibility so necessary for sustaining nonviolent resistance. At the same time, nonviolence became a critical part of the churches' proclamation of the Gospel.

The question may be asked whether nonviolence was more successful in these situations because they were all internal struggles rather than disputes between nations. In the instances we have examined, nonviolent resistance may have been more sustainable than in other possible situations for two reasons. First, during these conflicts no other nation intervened directly on behalf of either side. Also, no other nation functioned as an external foe which would have had the effect of refocusing the issue as "defending the nation" and of precipitating violence once nationalistic fervor was stirred. (Of course, there were plenty of candidates for *internal* "enemies of the people" who were common targets of regime violence. Yet the people did not take up arms, largely because of the efforts of the churches to prevent violence between Poles, between Germans, and between Filipinos).

Although these cases of successful nonviolent resistance involved internal rather than international disputes, there is no reason why the factors in their success cannot be applied to international conflicts as well. In Poland, East Germany, and in the Philippines the proponents of nonviolence were concerned with human liberation but were unwilling to wage a war of national liberation. Success in each case depended on developing the grassroots cooperation of many people who had learned patience.

Especially in Poland and in East Germany, the movements were committed to processes of social reconstruction rather than to immediate political victories.

To a considerable degree, nonviolent resistance has shown itself to be an effective strategy. Of course, cases such as Tiananmen Square could be cited in which nonviolent resistance was brutally crushed. Nonviolent resisters cannot be assured that their efforts will produce successful outcomes any more than war strategists can. However, the convictions which ground nonviolent resistance run considerably deeper than questions of success or failure. From Gandhi to Walesa, nonviolent resisters have emphasized their desire to defeat evil, not to defeat other people. They have sought not to humiliate their adversaries but to win them over. They have maintained that they are not in possession of the whole truth and that their adversary too has a truth to contribute. Their conviction of injustice remains strong, but they do not hold that their position is infallible. They are not willing to kill their adversaries, since to do so would in effect kill their own quest for truth. By showing respect for adversaries they hope to provide time in which their adversaries may see the evil of their ways and choose to change. Whether or not that will happen no one can know ahead of time. The tremendous challenge of nonviolent resistance is whether it can find practitioners with sufficient courage, faith, and good will to respond to adversaries in this way. That there are such virtuous people is abundantly clear. I offer one more historical account of such people.

In 1944, Daniel Trocmé had come to Le Chambon, a village in southcentral France, to be part of a dangerous mission. Trocmé came at the invitation of his cousin, pastor Andre Trocmé, to help in the care of Jewish children hidden in the area in defiance of Nazi deportation orders. The Christians of Le Chambon, descendants of Huguenots long persecuted by the Catholic majority in France, had dedicated themselves to rescuing several thousand Jews during the years 1941-1944. To the disgust of nearby French resistance forces, the Chambon-

naise refused to resort to violence in carrying out their operation because of the Gospel command of love of neighbor and
because they believed that even their adversaries were capable
of redemption. In a letter to his parents, Daniel Trocmé wrote:
"Le Chambon is something of a contribution to the reconstruction of the modern world."[40] "Reconstructing the modern
world" may have seemed then (and now) to be pretentious, if
not quixotic; yet the Chambonnaise saved the lives of several
thousand Jews and offered at least a flicker of hope that courageous and "righteous Gentiles" (as the Jewish people later
called them) still existed. Their world was in need of reconstruction and they provided an alternative to the falsehood and
violence of Nazism and the fear, apathy, and complicity it
bred. Only a short distance from where Albert Camus wrote
The Plague, his allegory about the power of courage and care in
dark times, the people of Le Chambon successfully resisted the
spiritual plague ravaging Europe.

One of several curiosities about the story of Le Chambon
was the fact that when Allied forces liberated the region, Nazi
troops did not take vengeance on Le Chambon as they had on
other villages known for their resistance. Almost two decades
later, the following explanation came to light. In the summer
of 1944, not long after the Allied landing at Normandy, Roger
Le Forestier, a doctor working in Le Chambon, was arrested by
the Gestapo and falsely accused of resistance activity. At his
trial before a German army tribunal, Le Forestier offered the
court an account of his Christian nonviolence. After the war,
the head of that tribunal, a Major Schmehling, acknowledged
that he was convinced of Le Forestier's innocence and managed to get him acquitted, but only with the provision that Le
Forestier agree to go to Germany to care for civilians wounded
in the air raids. Schmehling also said that as a Catholic he understood Le Forestier's commitment to the Gospel. The
German officer told Andre Trocmé many years later that the
doctor's Christian convictions had so moved him that he had

40. Daniel Trocme's letter is quoted by Pierre Sauvage in his documentary film
about Le Chambon, "Weapons of the Spirit" (1987).

dissuaded his superiors from sending a Nazi legion into Le Chambon. Trocmé quotes Schmehling as saying: "I told [SS Col.] Metzger that this kind of resistance had nothing to do with violence, nothing to do with anything we could destroy with violence."[41] Le Forestier's witness may well have saved the village of Le Chambon, although he nonetheless became one of the two martyrs of Le Chambon, murdered by Nazi collaborators en route to Germany. The other martyr was Daniel Trocmé, arrested by the Gestapo in a raid on his home for Jewish boys and murdered alongside thousands of Jews at Maidanek concentration camp in April 1945.

Although the story of Le Chambon offers no definitive proof of the efficacy of nonviolent resistance, it does suggest that a power greater than any human power may be at work in those who attempt to live faithfully to the Gospel call of love and peace. Does it not seem that the heart of an "enemy," Major Schmehling, was changed by the witness offered by Roger Le Forestier and the rest of the good people of Le Chambon?

The actions and convictions examined in this chapter all involved nonviolent resistance. None of the practioners involved considered themselves absolute pacifists. Nor were they utopians. Nonviolent resistance will continue to achieve successes without making naive claims about eliminating all violence. It is clear that the kind of pacifism we witness in nonviolent resistance is not "sectarian" in the sense that James Johnson identifies earlier Christian sectarian pacifists. Indeed, proponents of nonviolent resistance would disagree with Johnson and other just-war proponents, for whom "violence is an instrument for good or evil, depending on how it is used, by whom, and for what ends. . . ."[42] Lech Walesa, Adam Mishnik, Cardinal Sin and his fellow bishops, and the Chambon-

---

41. Quoted in Philip Hallie, *Lest Innocent Blood Be Shed* (New York: Harper and Row, 1979), 245.

42. James Johnson, *The Quest for Peace*. 281.

naise witnessed too much of the destructive effects of violence to be so trusting of its efficacy.

In 1984, historian Bohdan Cywinski reflected on what had transpired in Poland:

> The essential aim of any project of renewal in the world by means of a moral renaissance is not so much the construction of an earthly paradise as the fact of restraining and disarming a rampant evil. In this defence of human life against the evil that threatens it, we can discern the ultimate meaning of those appeals to brotherhood, solidarity, freedom and human dignity . . . . The encounter with contemporary evil of an exceptionally aggressive nature awoke in Poland the will to renewal and inclined a large number of people to renounce self-interest in order to defend themselves against the suppression of human rights and against the abasement of human dignity. Their witness will become even more powerful when it moves others to defend the same values, common to us all, in all the diversity of the actual situations which confront us in our own days.[43]

Someone once observed that Poland had the spiritual capacity to save the world from itself.[44] The compliment seems well-deserved by Poles and by all those everywhere who have worked for peace in a similar fashion.

---

43. Quoted in Craig, 313.

44. The observation was made to Mary Craig, 17.

Questions for Reflection

1. Why do you think that oppressive situations often contain the seeds of spiritual and moral renewal?

2. The Catholic Church, Lech Walesa, and Solidarity all protested against injustices in Poland. In what sense were they committed to more than "winning," i.e., "defeating" the political authorities?

3. Each of the movements described above was an internal rather than an international struggle. Do you think nonviolent resistance can be applied with equal effectiveness in international disputes? Why or why not?

4. Nonviolent resistance has been used especially by groups who have little military capability. In what sense is this a case of "strength in weakness"?

5. What would motivate U.S. citizens to embrace nonviolent methods even though the U.S. does not face an external military threat?

CHAPTER EIGHT

The Peacemaking Church

Introduction

The world order was changing dramatically as we entered the last decade of this millennium. But there were few signs that it was becoming less violent. Iraq invaded Kuwait and a coalition of nations led by the U.S. responded with a massive show of force. In the wake of the break-up of the Soviet Union, ethnic conflict exploded in the Balkans. Croatians established an independent state. Bosnian Muslims established Boznia-Herzegovina. Fearful Bosnian Serbs seized the vast military hardware of former Yugoslavia and used it to expel or kill thousands of Muslims and Croats. Croats attacked Muslim villages. Ethnic warfare claimed the lives of as many as two hundred and fifty thousand Croatians, Muslims, and Serbs — people who had lived in relative peace for many years. In Somalia, rival clans waged a fierce civil war while thousands of Somalis starved.

As the sole superpower, the U.S. has struggled to define its role. Its natural impulse was to function as global policeman. But seeking to quell international violence has not proven easy, as well-armed groups thwart our efforts to stop the killing and other human rights violations. The assumption that we can effectively respond to violence with superior violence, often revealing our characteristic impatience and arrogance, is being challenged. (A U.S. columnist recently chided "the boundlessness of American military obligation.") Given the massive defeat we so recently inflicted on Iraq, it is remarkable how quickly we are beginning to see our limitations in arresting worldwide violence.

The loss of U.S. confidence in dealing with violence abroad may be correlated to our inability to deal with the explosion of violent crime at home. In 1992, the U.S. reported 37,000 homicides. The U.S. Center for Disease Control now includes homicide as one of the top ten causes of death in America. The rise in domestic battery and neglect and abuse of children is so dramatic that our social and preventive services and court systems are overwhelmed. The challenge of containing violence abroad is now exceeded by the challenge of making peace in our homes, streets, and neighborhoods. What Thomas Merton predicted 25 years ago has come true: we have awakened to fire and violence in our own front yards.[1]

Theologian Bernard Häring challenges us to see violence as a pathological condition affecting all of us. Violence is now spreading through the body politic like a virus. Although the contagion continues to strike the marginalized poor and minorities most often, it has also increasingly begun to destroy at random. The disease has suddenly appeared in "happy marriages" and "good families" all around us. The disease has far outrun the capacity of a few specialists to cure. We cannot leave the problem of violence to the experts; therapists, social workers, judges, law enforcement officers, activists and church leaders cannot alone stem the spread of the disease. The only remedy for the disease is a long-term healing process in which

---

1. Thomas Merton foresaw that the violence of our war-making abroad and the patterns of racism at home would eventually overtake us: "We need not be surprised if we wake up one day and find fire and violence in our own front yards here in America." (*Thomas Merton on Peace*, Gordon Zahn, Ed., xxvii.) Merton told the Kerner Commission that the cause of the race riots of the late 1960s lay "not in some esoteric groups but in the culture itself, its extreme individualism and competitiveness, its inflated myth of virility and toughness, its overwhelming preoccupation with power. . . . If we live in what is essentially a culture of overkill, how can we be surprised that there is violence in it?" Ibid., xxxix.

we assist one another. Perhaps Camus's allegorical novel, *The Plague,* describes our situation and our options. In his story the entire city of Oran is under quarantine, leaving its citizens two options: either they can isolate themselves, hoping to evade the mysterious disease, or they can commit themselves to work for a cure and to nurse those stricken with it back to health. At this point in our history, Americans — and among them the rank and file of its churches, synagogues, and mosques — confront the plague of violence with similar choices. We can choose to live as if we were magically immune and the disease irrelevant. Or we can join those who seek a cure for the problem that effects us so greatly that we acknowledge it as *our* problem.

Fr. Häring urges Christians to a three-fold response. In the national political arena, Christians should seek to win over public opinion for finding nonviolent solutions to conflicts at all levels; in their local communities Christians should explore nonviolence and train themselves in nonviolent conflict resolution; at the level of faith, Christians must affirm that redemption from violence is possible.

This chapter concludes our discussion of Christian responses to conflict by exploring each of these responses to violence. In the course of doing so, we recap the previous discussions about the future of the just-war doctrine, about the nature of pacifism, and the practical possibilities of nonviolent resistance.

1. Passing on a Peace Tradition

A look at the past thirty years of Catholicism reveals stirrings of hope that the Church is preaching and practicing peace. In 1963, Pope John XXIII issued his encyclical "Peace on Earth," in which he declared that " . . . it is hardly possible to imagine that in the atomic era war could be used as an instrument of justice."[2] Two years later the Second Vatican Council issued the modern Church's strongest condemnation of war. For the U.S. Church, the 1960s was dominated by two painful

---

2. Pope John XXIII, *Pacem in Terris,* 127.

events: the civil rights struggle at home and the Vietnam conflict abroad. Both offered painful lessons for the Church, lessons sometimes taught by laity and religious courageous
enough to raise their voices and take a stand. Several groups
of U.S. Catholics opposed to the war emerged in this period.

In 1962, Eileen Egan, affiliated with the Catholic Worker
Movement, founded PAX, a peace organization with the mission of persuading the Catholic hierarchy to broaden and
deepen the Church's peace witness. Included in the political
agenda of PAX was passage of federal legislation to secure the
right of selective conscientious objection.

In 1963, a group of Catholics attempted to establish a U.S.
section of Pax Christi, the international Catholic peace organization established in 1945 by French Bishop Pierre-Marie Théas
and a group of French lay Catholics with the mission of praying for Germany, France's great adversary, and of working for
international reconciliation in war-torn Europe. Although Pax
Christi had twice received papal blessings and in 1963 was pre-
sided over by Belgian Cardinal Bernard Alfrink, the attempt to
organize an American chapter faltered for lack of a U.S. bishop
to serve as sponsor, a requirement of Pax Christi/International.

In those years, small groups of Catholic lay people,
priests, and religious had joined the struggle to bring peace in
the midst of the escalating Vietnam war. Their strength and
inspiration came from such peace advocates as Dorothy Day
and other members of the Catholic Worker movement and
from Trappist monk Thomas Merton, a leading spiritual writer.
(Day and some Catholic Workers were pacifists; Merton was
not.) In 1964, Daniel and Philip Berrigan helped to establish
the Catholic Peace Fellowship "to develop a theology of peace
with emphasis on the principles and techniques of nonviolent
resistance . . . and a vision of church that is peacemaking to its
very core."[3] The CPF also sought to educate Catholics on the
moral issues surrounding the war, including the issue of the
injustice of the draft system and the right of selective conscien-

---

3. Catholic Peace Fellowship statement of mission, 1966.

tious objection. Their goal was to broaden Catholic resistance to the Vietnam war. The membership of PAX and CPF diminished sharply after the war. But their legacy was a Catholic resistance wing, a small but dedicated group of Catholics who challenged the Catholic Church to confront racism at home, imperialism abroad (and particularly in Latin America), and the frenzied nuclear arms race between the superpowers. They forced the issue of just-war to centerstage. They brought pacifism home to the Church.[4]

In 1968, the majority of the U.S. bishops agonized over what to say to about the War as its violence spiraled out of control and anger over it spilled into the streets of America. But they did not speak out against it. Eventually the bishops were influenced by the Catholic Worker Movement, Merton, the handful of Catholic conscientious objectors, and the PAX and CPF activism—and by the course that the war itself was taking. Finally, in 1971 they raised their corporate voice, urging "our nation's leaders . . . to bring the war to an end with no further delay."[5] Though far from being a prophetic voice, the Bishops finally took what historian David O'Brien has called "an historic . . . and courageous step" that marked a turning point for the American Catholic Church.[6]

Twelve years later, their pastoral letter on the threat posed by the nuclear arms race proved to be a catalyst for public policy discussion and an aid to many in forming their consciences on issues of war and peace. Suddenly within the Catholic Church there was a groundswell of concern to reduce the threat of nuclear war. Bishops from around the world issued pastoral letters (including the Irish, French, German, Dutch, and Japanese episcopal conferences and England's

---

4.   David O'Brien credits the activities of Catholic peace activists with a revival of pacifism and a renewed interest in applying the just-war tenets to international conflicts. See "American Catholic Opposition to the Vietnam War: A Preliminary Assessment," in *War or Peace?*, 141-142.

5.   National Conference of Catholic Bishops, "Resolution on Southeast Asia" (Washington, D.C.: U.S. Catholic Conference, 1971.)

6.   David O'Brien, "American Catholic Opposition," 131.

Archbishop of Canterbury). Pope John Paul II has become a passionate witness for peace and critic of militarism.

What impact have peace activists and bishops had on the broader U.S. Catholic Church? The peace movements, peace "actions," and protests organized by small groups of Catholics challenged other Catholics. Their methods frequently involved direct confrontation intended to induce discomfort in others so that they would confront moral issues, search their consciences, and make responses. Their efforts to be prophetic did not always have their intended effect. While history has rendered a largely negative judgment on the Vietnam War, in 1971 many U.S. Catholics remained unconvinced of the position their bishops had taken, especially when the personal character of the protestors was less than "peaceful." Rather than convert many middle-class Catholics to the cause, a backlash occurred in which all listening stopped as the shouting increased. Like any other movements, peace movements are not always comprised of peace-filled people. In their zeal, people often become desperate, lack discipline, and succumb to self-righteousness. Thomas Merton, supporter to many in the Catholic peace movement, took a very negative view of the tactics of some in the movement and urged instead "patient, constructive, and pastoral work, rather than acts of defiance which antagonize the average person without enlightening him."[7]

Many U.S. bishops have become strong advocates of peace. Seventy of them are now among the 20,000 members of Pax Christi/USA that was finally established in 1973. In 1988 the bishops issued a follow-up report on their 1983 peace pastoral. In it they acknowledged the new hurdles in the progress toward disarmament. Although they believed that their pastoral letter had played a useful educational role among Catholics, they also recognized that working for peace required more than merely addressing policy-makers and those most likely to influence policy. Working for peace also required more than merely reiterating church teaching. Instead, they declared,

---

7. Quoted by Gordon Zahn, in *Thomas Merton on Peace*, xxxiv.

"The whole Church is called to become a *peacemaking church*, to 'form people capable of being true artisans of peace,' in the words of Pope John Paul II."[8] The bishops understood the need for the Catholic peace movement to advocate and educate for peace during peace time if it is to have any influence in resolving conflicts during times of crisis. The question remains: how is the Church to do that?

Peace activists and episcopal leaders either alone or together cannot create or sustain a peacemaking church. Bishops will continue to attempt to influence public policy. But their first role remains that of teachers of the faith who will help people to develop awareness of the moral dimensions of politics. The seeds they sow will be harvested in Christians working for justice and peace through their many lay vocations and associations. There are several ways in which the church can help to form peacemakers. The capacity for peacemaking emerges centrally from the liturgical life of the church. In the Catholic mass, Jesus' words of peace are spoken again ("My peace I leave with you, my peace I give to you") and worshippers exchange a gesture of peace with one another. From there it is intended to be carried with each participant. An Irish priest, Fr. Emmanual McCarthy, has suggested as an addition to the eucharistic prayer: "On the night before Jesus *rejected violence and* died, he broke bread and gave it to his disciples, saying, 'This is my Body.'" "Preaching the Word" should involve pastors addressing biblical texts that deal with peace and war, and echoing the biblical call to put aside violence. Many are reluctant to do so, afraid that they may sound too political and create controversy.

In addition to hearing the Words of scripture, we need to hear the testimony of early Christian communities, and also of Christians in our own time. We need to hear the stories of Polish and Filipino Catholics, German Lutherans and Baptists, and French Huguenots of Le Chambon (supported by American Quakers). These will help us see how we are to be the peace-

---

8. National Conference of Catholic Bishops, *Building Peace: A Pastoral Reflection on the Response to The Challenge of Peace* (Washington, D.C.: U.S. Catholic Conference, 1988), par. 12.

making church in our own cultural contexts. They will renew our hope in the power of Christians to turn enemies into friends and to overcome violence with nonviolence. These are the stories the Christian communities need to tell and hear in order that they may be reaffirmed in the powerful presence of grace in our world. Imagine what might happen if the churches of the U.S. were to sponsor an annual event similar to the "ten days of peace" sponsored by the churches of East Germany.

Pastoral letters issued from the "top" only begin the process of Christian education and formation. Gathering the faithful to deepen their understanding of the tradition and to clarify their own convictions is essential. The object of such education is not to create a uniform Catholic point of view, but to empower Catholics to make sound moral judgments and to find ways of putting their convictions into practical programs of action. For the past sixty years, the Catholic Worker Movement has welcomed thousands of people to its Friday evening programs aimed at what Peter Maurin called "clarification of thought." Even though American Catholics have over the years become increasingly better educated, reflection on faith and practice has lagged. As a church, there is great need for "clarification of thought" among Catholics regarding the traditions of just-war and pacifism. Are many Catholics familiar with just-war criteria? Is the notion of "proportionality" in armed conflict part of their moral awareness? Are concepts such as "just cause," "last resort," and "noncombatant immunity" sufficiently intelligible to influence moral judgment? Is pacifism well understood? For most people pacifism is only a vague notion. How many people understand its moral basis and recognize its fidelity to the Gospels?[9] How many see both traditions as part of a consistent pro-life stance within Catholicism?

---

9. In his examination of pacifism, Richard Miller illustrates the varieties of pacifism among contemporary Catholics. He challenges Catholic communities to consider what elements of pacifism ought to be affirmed as essential aspects of a Catholic peace ethic. Miller lists a "set of distinctions useful for refining the moral framework in which pacifism typically operates" and challenges the Catholic community to reconsider pacifism as an authentic Christian option. Miller lists ten contested issues to guide a critical reconsideration of pacifism: 1. does

Ideas have the power to capture and move us. From 1928-1968, The Catholic Association for International Peace was an identifiable community of U.S. Catholic intellectuals interested in fostering international security, cooperation, and peace. While they were never advocates of pacifism and even had an unbroken record in supporting U.S. war involvement, they were nonetheless interested in making a contribution to peacemaking. Where are their successors today? Some can be found on a few Catholic college and university campuses teaching peace and justice curricula. Ironically, their numbers, like those of programs in peace studies, are considerably smaller than the number of ROTC programs on Catholic campuses.

The church has a universal identity and mission. As a transnational community, it must be the body of Christ that bursts parochial boundaries of race, ethnicity and nationality in service to the world. Christians must recognize the bond between them that must melt the enmities that fracture Christian unity and spawn intrareligious violence.

2. "Make Me an Instrument of Your Peace"

Thomas Merton alerted us to some of the qualities of our culture that have contributed to violence and have made it difficult for us to resolve conflicts. A discussion of violence in our culture may seem to diverge from the central topic of this book, the use or nonuse of military force to resist injustice. Some may argue that whatever connections exist between the

---

it involve an absolute or relative condemnation of war?; 2. is it withdrawalist or transformationist regarding existing political systems?; 3. is pacifism seen as an act of self-sacrifice or more as a means of effecting reconciliation between antagonists?; 4. is pacifism a universal imperative or a "higher ethic" of a few?; 5. is its method non-resistance or nonviolent resistance?; 6. is it oriented toward civil disobedience or defense against external aggression?; 7. would its practitioners violate only unjust laws?; 8. does it advocate submitting to punishment or evading punishment?; 9. is the pacifist's method persuasion or coercion?; 10. does it advocate conditional or unconditional exemption from military service? *Interpretations in Conflict*, 82.

use of violence for political objectives and unsanctioned use of violence in homes and streets are too indirect and that consideration of the latter kind of violence is not helpful here. I will argue that it is helpful to address nonmilitary violence, for the reason that the two kinds of violence have common traits. At the very least, it is hard to imagine that persons with very limited capacity for resolving conflict interpersonally will be able to contribute to the capacity of their community to restrict its use of violence or engage in nonviolent ways. Certainly it is relevant to peacemaking to inquire how we can raise a generation of people able to resolve conflict without recourse to violence.[10] Whether among neighborhood gangs or in international negotiations, respecting other human beings and knowing how to handle conflict are essential.

The question before us is how we can do better, especially for the sake of our children? How can we raise them to be peaceful people, creative and confident enough to resolve conflicts without recourse to violence? The spiritual and psychological capacity for nonviolence begins in early childhood. The "inner work" of peacemaking is a life-long process that has its decisive origins in our early years. As children and adolescents we are influenced in ways that will later predispose us either toward violence or toward its healing. Erik Erikson's description of the stages of early childhood and adolescent development make it clear that these years of "people building" are critical for acquiring essential psychological strengths. Let us consider three such strengths.

First, the experience of being unconditionally loved is the basis on which a child's sense of self-worth will become firmly established. Adults who only bestow affection on a child as reward or withhold it as punishment plant seeds of anxiety rather than nurture a deeply-rooted self-esteem. Children who feel that they must win the acceptance of others often doubt their own worth. They have poor self-esteem and are deeply

---

10. I credit Mr. James Keane for this point.

anxious that they will be rejected by others. Such children grow up regarding other people as potential threats.

Second, children who are affirmed develop an expanded self-confidence. They are not just subject to the will of others but develop the necessary capacity to play an active role in the direction of their own lives. Without such personal power, children feel a sense of powerlessness. Having been dominated by others, they will seek means of relating to others in ways that are also dominating.

Third, encouraging children to be creative rather than to conform contributes to their self-assurance and self-esteem. Children who are tightly controlled and made to conform often become controlling and conforming adults; it is not easy to foster creativity in others when one's own has been discouraged. Assurances of personal worthiness, competence, and creativity free the life courses of adults of compulsive attempts to establish worthiness and competence often manifested in forms of intense competitiveness, controlling behavior, suspicion, resentment, blame, and distrust of others. Healthy psychological development allows people to form bonds of trust, to be sensitive to the needs of others, and to be altruistic in orientation. Their responses are not defensive and manipulative; instead, they can negotiate life's inevitable conflicts, rather than erect barriers or lash out. From their own sense of worthiness, competence, and creativity comes the capacity to see and affirm the good of others and even to convert adversaries into friends.

Adult anger that is directed toward children or that children witness has a powerful effect upon them. The emotion of anger is not necessarily a destructive thing. Anger may be a legitimate protest that one's needs are being ignored. It may function to help others listen and respond to those needs. But anger may be destructive as well, closing down communication and demeaning others. When "bigger" people direct their anger at "littler" people, it is often done so with the demand that the latter agree with the views of the "bigger people" and obey their will. No one wants to be subjected to the anger of others. Littler people — including children — must find ways to protect themselves from the anger of bigger people. Children learn to cope with chronic anger in adults by repressing the many negative feelings it can engender in them. With angry adults "on them," children may either attempt to flee, block it out, counter-attack, or take it out on somebody else. They disengage, never learning to express the full range of their own emotions of anger, hope, and affection which are needed to develop a healthy sense of self-esteem. They carry into their adolescence and adulthood distrust of others, deeply unsure of their own goodness and competence. They feel helpless and have little resources for dealing with conflict situations.

Whether they are meek and fearful adults or very angry adults, their ability to form relationships based on mutuality, honesty, and to care for others has been harmed. Especially for men, the inability to identify strong feelings such as fear, disappointment, humiliation, and jealousy can quickly push them into anger, rage, and violence.[11]

In adulthood, the inner work continues. Learning to live nonviolently is a process of rooting out our insecurities and allowing healing to take place in and through us. As noted in the first chapter of this study, the virtues are a way of talking about the emergence of positive powers of peacemaking. Faith is present in our deepening trust in God's presence to bring about the good. When civil rights demonstrators sang "We shall overcome" what they were saying was "this is God's day, and whatever happens to us, God will overcome." Hope is alive when our quickening imaginations see possibilities rather than succumb to a sense of powerlessness. Love allows us to truly see others as people with needs such as our own and to become healers.

Erikson identifies the desire for integrity as the final stage of personal development. Integrity means rejecting what is not truthful in the way the world has organized itself and makes its claims upon us. In addition to intellectual recognition, truth demands active commitment. Thomas Merton observed that the precious few European communities who rejected and re-

---

11. Psychologists have referred to this tendency as the "male emotional-funnel system."

sisted Nazism were capable of doing so because they took fundamental truths seriously. They saw evil for what it truly was and they saw what was entailed in putting their own lives at the service of the truth. There was no gap between what they knew and how they stood for that truth.

The inner work leads to the outer work of resolving conflict by many means. It calls for critical reevaluation of our patterns of production and consumption that encourage greed, competitiveness, disregard for the environment, and the diversion of immense human and economic resources to policies and implements of destruction. It calls for the acknowledgment of our complicity with violence and for attempts to renounce our reliance upon violence. Is there violence that we must still say No to? Must we still be working on our own recovery from violence by embracing a life of nonviolence? Or do we continue to believe that violence can be effectively and safely "managed"? Do we sanction its use for securing the "common good" and pursuing the national interests while at the same time repudiating its use in private self-interest? What drives both uses of violence is the belief that it is the only effective recourse we have. Especially for those who have been subjected to a violent living environment, violence may come to be seen as the only effective means of asserting themselves, defending themselves, and surviving. Until and unless nonviolent means of meeting interests and solving disputes are seen as more effective, violence will reign supreme.

We must question the assumption that there is good violence and bad violence. Violence crushes the human spirit and digs deep chasms that prevent us from joining the human community. At this point we fear for our children, lamenting the amount of violence they are exposed to and alarmed at their violent behavior. But let us consider just how they are being raised and trained to behave by parents who will be the first to repudiate "bad violence."

The first way in which adults teach nonviolence is by modeling other ways of resolving conflicts. If violence has a hold over the lives of adults, it will be impossible for them to raise their children otherwise. If violence holds fascination for adults — and the profitability of violence in the mass media makes that clear enough — it will surely be the same for their children. The question remains: how are we, as adults, rejecting violence?[12]

We lament the lost childhoods of so many children. They all seem to grow up too fast: they are becoming like us sooner and surer than ever before. If their world is violent it is no surprise: they have seen how the adult world behaves. They are not a strange mutation but the convergence of many features of past generations. We blame them but we must also grieve for them; the grief to which so many of them are coming must give us new resolve to present them with alternatives to the violent culture all about them. The family remains our first school of violence and nonviolence, of conflict and conflict resolution. Initiatives by parents and by other sources of authority in the lives of children are critically important.

Fortunately there are hopeful signs that children are learning alternatives to violence. Schools are taking the lead in our society in teaching young children how to deal with conflict. The process begins with the awareness that conflict is an inevitable part of our lives. Students are aided to develop the skills necessary to work through conflict in ways that lead to greater mutual understanding rather than greater alienation between disputants. By learning new interpersonal skills, children can reconceptualize conflict: it is no longer only a contest of wills between adversaries in which one of them successfully asserts will and power over the other with the other losing both in terms of whatever was at stake and in terms of a bruised ego.

---

12. The Center for Media and Values has created a multimedia literacy program to educate children and adults on media and violence. For information on the program, "Beyond Blame: Challenging Violence in the Media," and on center membership and the establishment of local chapters, write to the Center for Media and Values, 1962 S. Shenandoah St., Los Angeles, CA, 90034.

Communication skills are at the heart of the process. Teaching conflict resolution begins with helping children learn how to listen well in order to understand the reality of another person and to appreciate the needs of that person. Children know how satisfying it is when someone "really listens" to them. In conflict situations, students voluntarily agree to sit down with a "peer mediator." The mediator helps both sides to express themselves without interruption and to hear as fully as possible the feelings and needs of the other. Knowing another's reality is knowing how they are feeling.

We do not easily perceive the feelings of others. They must be able to tell us. Children are learning how to state their feelings and needs directly rather than blaming others for the present conflict. While the conflict may surely involve failure and fault, focusing on one's own feelings and needs rather than on the failures of others opens the way to more successful conflict resolution for several reasons. First, stating needs specifies what a successful resolution must address. Second, blaming leads to defensive reactions, denial, or blaming back. Third, assigning blame suggests that only one person holds the key to successfully resolving a conflict.

To resolve a conflict a solution must be found that satisfies both sides. Discovering such a solution can be difficult for both children and adults. Adult authorities may impose solutions on children, either interceding in squabbles before children can work them out themselves or refusing to give up any control by negotiating with their children over any issue — family rules, for instance. Allowing children to generate their own solutions helps them take control and responsibility in important ways. Adults, too, may frequently imagine only very limited solutions to a conflict. Successful conflict resolution requires the use of imagination in order to generate a variety of solutions from which a list of potential solutions may be refined. From several possible solutions emerge those which both sides find agreeable and workable.

Training in conflict resolution and management teaches children that they can solve conflicts and that the process of working through a conflict builds bridges to others and enhances their own self-worth more than "fight or flight" alternatives do. Understanding, empathy, self-disclosure, and confidence are the result. The outcome of conflict need not be painful and destructive but may contribute to growth in mutual respect. Supporting such training is an important dimension of the religious and moral education which the churches must provide to their young. It is part of the peacemaking task of the church.

Churches have begun to recognize the need for ministries to help heal our domestic violence. But as a culture we seem far from recognizing the link between the violence that our culture condemns and the violence it condones. We sanction violence in pursuit of the public interest and national causes; we punish violence (with violence!) used in pursuit of private interests. But the cross-over now occurs routinely: violence that "works" in one sphere is increasingly resorted to in the other. People who see violence as the characteristic way that those in power respond to conflict will naturally choose it to respond to their conflicts. Violence is the school in which they have been formed. Nonviolence is the alternative school that Christians, in cooperation with others, must establish.

Conclusion

We have considered two morally principled responses to conflict which Christians have historically made. Although they are different responses, they both seek to protect other human beings from harm. Those who support the principles of just-war realize that war is, at best, a blunt instrument for resolving conflict and restoring peace. War may not directly bring about peace, but may reestablish international order and respect for human rights — conditions that may be necessary to achieve peace.[13] Those of a pacifist persuasion see the use of force as compounding conflicts rather than resolving them. Ad-

---

13. Just-war theorists make this point. For example, see James Johnson, "The Just War Idea and the Ethics of Intervention," 12.

dressing the Bosnian conflict, Diana Francis, former president of the International Fellowship of Reconciliation, elaborated on that point of view, arguing that,

> to succumb to the arguments for armed intervention — that is, for the use of methods which involve principally killing and destruction, for action which makes one side less than human, no longer worthy of the human right to life and dignity, no longer even worthy of trial before execution — is to support the notion that human rights and decency can be upheld by acts of lawlessness and barbarity. It is to accept the logic of trial by violence.[14]

What conclusions can we draw about the future of both traditions? Given the escalation of all manners of violence in our times, from domestic assault to ethnic and ideologically motivated warfare, we can first state the obvious: more effective ways of resolving conflict must be discovered. Whether warfare will be more restrictive in its ends and means, and thus less destructive, remains to be seen. The more stringent interpretation of just-war criteria proposed in Chapter Five would help. The growth of nonviolent means of conflict resolution offers genuine hope for the future. Let us say a final word about each tradition.

John Courtney Murray wrote that the just-war tradition has three important functions. First, it seeks to limit the outbreak and devastating consequences of war. During the Persian Gulf War, concern for direct assaults on civilians did play a limiting role in the devising of military tactics. But there was little indication that the experience produced deeper sensitivity among Americans. Video images of laser-guided missiles became occasions to celebrate the latest in military technology. Iraqi casualties were counted only in units of destroyed military equipment. Little criticism was heard about the war's toll on either Iraqi civilians or soldiers. While war often has a profound sensitizing effect of those who directly experience it,

---

14. Diana Francis, "If We Want to Stop Killing," *Reconciliation International* Vol. 8 No.2 (Summer, 1993), 4.

those removed from war in space or time often do not learn the lesson.

Secondly, the just-war theory offers us a common moral language with which to debate important moral issues in the public forum. If the people are to influence their country's foreign policy, it is essential that there be public debate in which they can be heard. Amid the continual tension between public openness and closed deliberations, the just-war criteria "set the right terms for public debate on war."[15] During the Gulf crisis, debate did occur. Yet at each stage of the unfolding crisis, important information was withheld from the public by the U.S. government. The Bush Administration concealed its dealings with Saddam Hussein prior to the invasion of Kuwait, it concealed its plans for large troop increases in the Gulf until after the Congressional elections in November 1990, and it suppressed news of Hussein's willingness to accept the U.N. Resolution to withdraw from Kuwait before the war broke out. Once the war began, news from the Gulf was censored more thoroughly than in any previous war in U.S. history. As a result, the American people were poorly informed about the crisis.[16]

Thirdly, just-war theory ought to provide individuals guidance in forming their consciences. Again, the media play an important role, by providing accurate information necessary to form judgments. Not only did the government manage what citizens learned about the Gulf conflict, but the media engaged in self-censorship in order to protect their ratings. Norman Solomon, a media analyst, argues that "the big media went along to get along with the war-makers," and points out that "no Federal agency forced the news media to rely on a narrow

---

15. John Courtney Murray, "Remarks on the Moral Problem of War" *Theological Studies* 20 (1959) 57.

16. For an account of the media's frustrations in covering the Gulf War, see John J. Fialka, *Hotel Warriors: Covering The Gulf War*, (Baltimore: Woodrow Wilson Center Press/ Johns Hopkins University Press, 1992) and John R. MacArthur, *Second Front: Censorship and Propaganda in the Gulf War* (New York: Hill and Wang, 1992).

range of pro-war analysts that dominated the networks and news pages. . . . "[17] As citizens we must assume greater responsibility for seeking nonviolent solutions for conflicts on all fronts.

While Christian pacifists can be found throughout the history of Christianity, the practice of conflict resolution and nonviolent resistance on a sizable social scale is a recent development. The stories of Christians who have undertaken these practices are little known because they are seldom reported. (In all fairness, it is difficult to find many nonviolent movements in the U.S. During the conflict in the Persian Gulf, none were able to effectively mobilize and present an alternative course of action.) But nonviolent alternatives often go unheralded. For example, in the Balkans, representatives from several national chapters of Pax Christi and the International Fellowship of Reconciliation labor to assist Muslims, Serbs, and Croats in living together peaceably. "Listening sessions" have been organized by U.S. church people in Serbian villages to heal divisions and maintain the peace between Serbs and Muslims. At least two dozen such initiatives have been undertaken by Christian groups advocating nonviolent solutions to the Balkan conflicts.[18]

Certainly, the churches have far to go in preparing Christians in the self-discipline required for the practice of nonviolence. Faith, hope, love, patience, and humility are slowly acquired. The Catholic bishops described the marks of the peacemaking church: continuous prayer for peace, education of its youth in the Gospel of peace, and pastoral support for church members to "become bearers of peace in their own situations."[19] Their point is clear: the peacemaking church is a re-

---

17. *New York Times*, May 24, 1991, A15. Solomon is co-author of *Unreliable Sources: A Guide to Detecting Bias in News Media* and an associate of Fairness and Accuracy in Reporting, a media watch group.

18. These peace efforts are little known in the U.S. and are more widely reported in the European media because of the activity of Peace Media Service, based in Amsterdam.

19. *Building Peace: A Pastoral Reflection on the Response to The Challenge of Peace.* Pars 13-14.

ality only insofar as its members are receiving and proclaiming the peace of Christ to the world.

Thirty years after World War II ended, Philip Hallie visited Le Chambon, France, to learn more about that community's nonviolent conspiracy to rescue Jews from Nazi occupiers. Impressed with the success of the nonviolent methods of the Chambonnaise, Hallie asked one of the pastors who had led the movement whether he thought nonviolence might have been successfully used by the Soviet Union to protect itself from the Germans. The pastor answered,

> No. They had to use violence then. It was too late for nonviolence. Both the Germans and the Russians . . . had to play out their terrible roles upon each other. Besides, nonviolence involves preparation and organization, methods patiently and unswervingly employed — the Russians knew nothing of this. Nonviolence must have deep roots and strong branches before it can bear the fruit it bore in Le Chambon. Nonviolence for them would have been suicide; it was too late.[20]

The pastor's reply is important for us to reflect upon as we conclude this study. If we are always preparing for war, it is quite likely we will play out "terrible roles upon each other" — and the just-war restraints will not stop us. To prevent this, we will need to be doing something else — forming creative nonviolent communities to stem the violence.

We began this book by observing how broad the concept of peace is. For believers, peace is a comprehensive goal because it is a call to transcend our fallen reality, to be renewed, and to prepare in the present for the fullness of the Kingdom of God yet to come. Because the peace of God is our destiny and fulfillment, there is no one thing to be done for peace. Instead, there is everything to do.

---

20. Hallie, *Lest Innocent Blood Be Shed*, 34-35.

For Further Thought and Action

1. What aspect of contemporary violence or nonviolence would be a timely subject for an evening of education and reflection in your congregation?

2. If you have school age children or grandchildren, are they currently learning conflict resolution skills in school? If not, consider exploring such programs and offering to help establish one.

3. Become aware of peacemakers in your community. For example, is there a local chapter of Pax Christi in your community? What concrete activity could you commit yourself to on behalf of peace?

Note to Educators

BOTH YOUNG PEOPLE AND ADULTS LEARN BY A VARIETY OF MEANS. Since our culture is visually oriented, the use of video material is especially useful to stimulate thinking and learning. The resources described here are recommended for use in conjunction with various parts of this book.

Practical experience through direct involvement in peace-making efforts greatly enhances the exploration of peace. Such activities also counteract the temptation to despair over the problems of war and violence. I especially recommend that educators explore local opportunities for students to be involved personally in activities and services that promote peace at home and abroad. I describe several resources to join in national efforts at the local level.

Modern War (Chapters Two-Five)

The documentary "War" is a provocative examination of modern war. Its 8 one-hour segments deal with the methods and impact of modern warfare, nuclear issues, the military profession and training, and the prospects for avoiding war.

Especially revealing is the segment entitled "Anybody's Son Will Do," that follows 18-year-olds through basic training and the process by which they are conditioned to kill. The series was produced by the National Film Board of Canada.

"Beyond Vietnam: Lessons Unlearned" is a documentary film by Steven Bentley, a Vietnam Veteran. Bentley describes his own odyssey as a young marine and the psychological effects of the war on him and many others. The film includes an examination of post-traumatic stress disorder, a universal phenomenon for those who fight wars. The film may be ordered by calling (207) 772-1603.

The short stories of Tim O'Brien convey an experience of the Vietnam War that rivals some of the best modern literary efforts to capture the experience of war. See especially *The Things They Carried* (Houghton Mifflin, 1990).

"Dear America: Letters Home from Vietnam" is a history of the Vietnam War told mainly through letters of American soldiers and medics. It is distributed by HBO and widely available for rental.

"The War We Left Behind" documents the effects of the Gulf War on Iraqi society. It was produced three months after the war. (See Chapter Four)

The Institute for Multi-Track Diplomacy is a group that works to resolve conflict in "hot spots" throughout the world through nongovernmental diplomatic initiatives. It publicizes its efforts in *PeaceBuilder*. For information write: IMTD, 1133 20th St. N.W., Suite 321, Washington, D.C. 20036.

Pacifism and Nonviolent Resistance (Chapters Six and Seven)

"Gandhi," the movie, is an excellent introduction to his life and to his great contributions to the practice of nonviolent social change.

"The Refusal" is a documentary about Franz Jaegerstaetter, an Austrian Catholic who refused induction into the army of the Third Reich and was executed by the Nazis. The film is available by writing to Pax Christi (see address below).

"Eyes on the Prize" is a PBS series on the U.S. civil rights movement. Its multiple segments cover the movement from the 1950s to the early 1980s. The first episode, "Awakenings: 1954-1956," documents the methods of nonviolent resistance first used by Dr. Martin Luther King, Jr. and the Montgomery movement. Other episodes examine the role of nonviolence in the unfolding civil rights movement and the criticisms to those methods offered by the younger generation of blacks. The last episode, "Back to the Movement," offers a retrospective review as well as a consideration of the future of race relations in this country.

"Weapons of the Spirit" is a documentary about the people of Le Chambon, France, who offered refuge to Jews fleeing Nazism during the Second World War. The story it tells refutes the often-heard criticism that nonviolent resistance could never have worked against the Nazis. The filmmaker is a Jew who was saved by the Christians of Le Chambon. First Run Features, 153 Waverly Place, New York, NY 10014.

Peacemaking (Chapter Eight)

The Catholic Worker movement continues to thrive in over 40 houses of hospitality throughout the U.S. Its members commit themselves to poverty in order to assist the nation's poor. They are assisted by many volunteers and always welcoming of more. Their commitment to nonviolence is visible in all of their work.

The Fellowship of Reconciliation, established in war-torn France 80 years ago, continues to seek nonviolent alternatives to war and to assist those suffering from war's effects. FOR's work and beliefs are publicized in *Fellowship*. For information write: Box 271, Nyack, NY 10969-0271.

Pax Christi USA is part of an international Catholic organization working for peace and disarmament. It is organized in state chapters in the U.S. For information write: 348 E. 10th St., Erie, PA 16503.

Programs teaching conflict resolution skills are increasingly being incorporated into primary and secondary school curricula. To learn about such programs contact the National Association for Mediation in Education, 205 Hampshire House, University of Massachusetts, Amherst, MA 01003. Very creative conflict resolution curricular materials for all grade levels are available from the Peace Education Foundation, 3550 Biscayne Blvd., Suite 400, Miami, FL 33139.

The Center for Media and Values offers videos and learning resources for different age groups to assist local communities and schools in counteracting violence in popular media. (For address, see Chapter Eight.)

Peacenet is a computer network on peace and environmental issues. It offers timely information on legislation, conferences, and the work of such organizations as Amnesty International. For membership write to the Institute for Global Communications, 18 Be Boom St., San Francisco, CA 94107 (415) 442-0220.

The Consortium on Peace Research, Education and Development (COPRED) offers academicians and activists an opportunity to share research and experiences. For information write: Institute for Conflict Analysis and Resolution, George Mason University, Fairfax, VA 22030.

Index

Abraham, 3
Acton, Lord, 31
Albright, Madelaine, 84
Alexis, Patriarch, 128
Alfrink, Bernard, Cardinal, 146
Aquinas, Thomas, 105
Aquino, Benigno, 129-30
Aquino, Corazon, 129-30, 133-35
Arendt, Hannah, 31, 35
Asiz, Foreign Minister, 28
Augustine, St., 2, 19-20, 36, 47, 97, 100, 104-5, 113

Baker, Secretary of State, 32, 42
Benedict XV, Pope, 90-91
Bentley, Steven, 165
Berrigan, Daniel and Philip, 110, 146
bishops: American. See U.S. Catholic Bishops; Belgian, 96; German, 96; Japanese, 96; Philippine, 130, 132-33, 135; Polish, 122, 135-36
Biden, Joseph, 34
Borisov, Aleksandr, 128
Brezhnev, Leonid, 121
Bush, George, vi, 21-23, 29-30, 34, 37, 41-42, 44, 46, 66, 75, 81, 160

Cahill, Lisa, 108
Camus, Albert, 139, 145
Childress, James, 47

Clauswitz, 78
Claver, Francisco, Bishop, 136
Clement of Alexandria, 99
Clinton, Bill, 84-86
Constantine, 98, 100
Cywinski, Bohdan, 118, 141

Dante, 101
Day, Dorothy, 93, 110, 146
Dowty, Alan, 34-35, 41-43, 50, 71

Egan, Eileen, 146
Enrile, Juan, 133-35
Erasmus, 101
Erikson, Erik, 152, 154

Francis, Diana, 159

Gandhi, Mohatma, 103, 114-15, 124, 138, 165
Glemp, Jozef, Cardinal, 121-22
Gorbachev, Mikhail, 126-27
Grotius, Hugh, 24-25, 29
Guelff, Richard, 64

Hallie, Philip, 162
Häring, Bernard, 2, 14-15, 144-45
Hehir, J. Bryan, 63-64
Hempel, Johannes, Bishop, 127
Hickey, James, Archbishop, 76
Hitler, Adolf, 93, 116, 136-37

Holmes, Robert, 115
Hussein, Saddam, viii, 21-22, 27-28, 30, 36-37, 40-42, 46, 48-49, 58, 60, 62, 65-66, 68, 70, 73, 81, 87, 160

Isaiah, 4

Jaegerstaetter, Franz, 93, 165
Jaruzelski, Wojciech, 122
Jesus Christ, 1, 4-7, 98
John, St., 11
John XXIII, Pope, 145
Johnson, James, 43, 47-48, 85-86, 87, 98-99, 101, 108-9, 140
John Paul II, Pope, 80-82, 89, 120-21, 148
Junghans, Helmar, 124, 126-27

Kelly, Thomas, 60
Keys, William, 66
King, Martin Luther, Jr., 11-12, 114-15, 124, 166
Kuron, Jacek, 120

Langan, John, 44, 62, 69, 76, 81-83
Laurel, Salvador, 130, 133
Law, Bernard, Cardinal, 76
Leo XIII, Pope, 90
Le Forestier, Roger, 139-40
Liber, Francis, 73
Lohfink, Norbert, 8
Lopez, George, 62, 73
Luther, Martin, 124

Mahoney, Roger, Archbishop, 23-24
Marcos, Ferdinand, 129-34
Marcos, Imelda, 129, 132
Marsilius of Padua, 101
Maurin, Peter, 150
McCaffrey, Barry, 69

McCarthy, Emmanuel, 149
McPeak, Merrill, 68, 70
Meehan, Francis X., 76-78
Merton, Thomas, 144, 146, 148, 151, 154
Metzger, Col., 140
Michnik, Adam, 120, 122, 140
Miller, Richard, 92, 97, 113-14
Moore, Royal N., 67
Moses, 3
Murray, John Courtney, 33, 159

Neal, Richard, 59-60

O'Brien, David, 147
O'Brien, Tim, 165
Origen, 99

Paul, St., 10, 11
Paul VI, Pope, 80
Perez de Quayar, Javier, 35
Pesch, Rudolf, 9
Pius XI, Pope, 91, 97
Pius XII, Pope, 26, 29, 31, 91
Popieluszko, Jerzy, 122
Powell, Colin, 67

Ramos, Fidel, 133-35
Ramsey, Paul, 53
Reagan, Ronald, vii
Roach, John, Archbishop, 23-24, 76
Roberts, Adam, 64
Ryan, John, Archbishop, 76

Sarah, 3
Schmehling, Major, 139-40
Schnackenburg, Rudolf, 6
Schwartzkopf, Norman, 55, 57-58, 64-65
Sharp, Gene, 115
Sin, Jaime, Cardinal, 129-32, 134, 140
Solomon, Norman, 160

Spaemann, Heinrich, 7
Stassen, Glen, 13, 128
Swoboda, Jorg, 127

Tertullian, 99
Thatcher, Margaret, 22
Théas, Pierre-Marie, Bishop, 146
Trocmé, Andre, 138
Trocmé, Daniel, 138-40

U.S. Catholic Bishops, vi, 1, 3, 5, 7, 9, 13-14, 24-26, 75, 79, 93-96, 111, 147-49

Vatican II, 78-80, 92-93, 97

de Vittoria, Francisco, 24, 29, 82

Walesa, Lech, 119-24, 138, 140
Walzer, Michael, 45, 53
Warden, John, 58
Weaver, Dorothy Jean, 6
Webster, William, 43
World Council of Churches, 18
Wyszynski, Stefan, Cardinal, 117-18, 121

Yeltsin, Boris, 128

Zahn, Gordon, 92, 110, 136